Miss Julie,

David Mamet Fan Club,

and Other Plays

towards a more open
dramaturgy —
 to Gordon with much
appreciation of your
expertise and for your help
throughout the years.
 Lance   Jan. 2000

Miss Julie,

David Mamet Fan Club,

and Other Plays

by

Lance Tait

with introductions by
Yvonne Shafer and Frank Hoff

Enfield Publishing
Enfield, New Hampshire

Published in 2000. First Printing.

Publishers Cataloging-in-Publication
  (Provided by Quality Books, Inc.)

Tait, Lance.
      Miss Julie, David Mamet Fan Club, and other
   plays / by Lance Tait ; with introductions by
   Yvonne Shafer and Frank Hoff. -- 1st ed.
      p. cm.
      CONTENTS: Miss Julie -- The Babysitter/Germany
   -- East play -- David Mamet fan club -- Jesus and
   the monkfish -- Behave, my sorrow -- Live free or
   die.
      ISBN: 0-9656184-9-8

      1. Experimental drama, American.   2. Mamet,
   David--Drama.   3. Strindberg, August, 1849-1912.
   Froken Julie.   I. Shafer, Yvonne, 1936-
   II. Hoff, Frank.   III. Title.

      PS3570.A326M57 2000   812'. 54
                            QBI99-1574

Printed in the U. S. A. by Morris Publishing, Kearney, NE

Published by Enfield Publishing,
P.O. Box 699, Enfield, NH 03748

Contents

Introduction

From earliest times of theatre people have been fascinated by realism on stage, even when the plays were essentially non-realistic. Medieval plays featured the decapitation of a saint whose head then bounced on the stage creating realistic miraculous fountains with each bounce. Shakespeare and his colleagues explored the qualities of ox blood and pig's blood to create the realistic illusion of blood on a supposedly wounded actor. Nevertheless, it is only in modern times that realism per se has come to have a grip—some would say a stranglehold—on Western theatre.

With the development of electricity, the painted perspectives, painted furniture on sets, even painted crowds on sets which had previously seemed realistic were revealed as nothing but a scene painter's attempt to create realism. Utilizing electricity, David Belasco created a wonderfully realistic change from evening to night to dawn in *Madame Butterfly*. In other plays he created the realistic impression of mountains, brought real horses on stage, and had real crowds with nursing mothers, sheep, dogs, children, etc. In one play a waitress flipped real pancakes on a real stove; in another a real cat crossed the stage, stretched, then raced toward the fireplace where it played with a ball of yarn. In yet another, the setting was actually a cheap room in a boarding house Belasco had purchased. His actors wore coats he had got from bums by trading his own coats. In this same time period audiences thrilled to *Uncle Tom's Cabin* with its realistic settings, Eliza's escape across the ice pursued by real bloodhounds, and the real horses pulling the carriage for Little Eva's first entrance. Even more amazing use of horses occurred in *Ben Hur* with four horses on treadmills pulling the racers in their carriages as the realistic panorama turned to give an impression of an actual race. Even the great John Barrymore was upstaged by a soda fountain with real fizz water that he dispensed in a turn of the century play.

Such excesses in a theatre utterly dominated by realism have been thoroughly described in A.N. Vardac's book, *Stage to Screen.* In this book he puts forth the idea that much of what the theatre technicians were straining to achieve was made unnecessary and weak by comparison with the development of the cinema. To many writers this was a glimmer of hope. Such movements as Symbolism, Futurism, Surrealism, and Expressionism were protests against the stultifying effects of realism on the imagination of writers and audiences. Aside from a brief period in the twenties, however, when Expressionism caught the fancy of audiences and critics, the cry for realism continued. It was strengthened by the development of interest in the theories of Stanislavski regarding realistic acting. As generations of actors moved into the study of realism as the ultimate in acting, it became more difficult for writers to present non-realistic plays with the appropriate acting styles. New plays that were non-realistic, such as Tennessee Williams' *Camino Real* with its Expressionistic devices and madcap action, were treated harshly by the critics, misunderstood by audiences, and were often complete failures.

Although mainstream drama in the United States has been realistic throughout the twentieth century, there have been many efforts to promote non-realistic drama. Early in the century many theatre groups were organized with the purpose of presenting a wide range of new playwriting in all styles. Winthrop Ames was an important producer whose approach was in strong contrast to that of Belasco. In 1912 he built the Little Theatre (now the Helen Hayes) with only 299 seats (in contrast to the large theatres with equipment for all types of realistic effects on stage) and there produced many plays that went against the demands for realistic playwriting. *The Terrible Meek* created a sensation with its retelling of the Crucifixion presented entirely in the dark, with only a few moments of light at the end revealing three figures on crosses and Mary kneeling on the ground. He introduced New York theatergoers to the fascination of Asian theatre with a modern retelling of an ancient Chinese drama, *The Flower of the Palace Han*. A reviewer praised the "strange grotesque dances of masked figures" and the non-realistic settings created by Chinese draperies in brilliant colors.

A few years later the Provincetown Players was created by playwrights Jig Cook and Susan Glaspell. Her imaginative plays were first presented in a tiny theatre on a wharf in Provincetown, Massachusetts and then in a small former stable in Greenwich Village in New York City. Her plays encompassed a range of styles including Expressionism. Her play *The People* brought forth characters from the subconscious of an exhausted, failing liberal newspaper editor, pleading with him to continue in his cause. In typical Expressionistic style the characters do not have realistic names—Glaspell herself played The Woman From Idaho. This play was criticized when it was written and later because the characters were not developed realistically. Even more criticism was heaped on her major work *The Verge* which was a notable failure in 1921. The play focused on a woman who was so oppressed by the frustration of trying to have a career and finding her own, individual way in the world that she ultimately, and willingly, slips into madness.

Working alongside Glaspell in the same theatres was the young playwright Eugene O'Neill. Although he worked in a variety of styles, his realistic plays *Long Day's Journey Into Night* and *Ah, Wilderness!* are most often produced today. To many actors and directors, however, his experiments with masks in *The Great God Brown*, his experimentation with interior monologues in *Strange Interlude*, and the use of Expressionism in such plays as *The Emperor Jones* have a great fascination and reveal the breadth of his imagination. Today audiences are once again being given the opportunity to see these early plays, many of which were condemned by critics, at the same theatre in which they were originally produced. Stephen Kennedy Murphy, Artistic Director of the Playwrights Theater of New York is presenting the entire range of O'Neill's plays.

Many other playwrights throughout the century have upheld the banner of non-realistic drama. In the 1950s Fay and Garson Kanin presented *Rashoman* which told the same story as seen through the eyes of four different viewers and participants. Critics and audiences responded enthusiastically to the Japanese tale and the non-realistic staging. One critic predicted that the future of American playwriting would be brighter if more attempts were made to incorporate the non-realistic staging used in Japanese theatre. Within a few years such Off-Broadway theatres as the Caffe Cino provided opportunities for non-realistic playwrights. In England, too, in recent years, many playwrights have turned away from realism. Peter Barnes, who was honored for such plays as *The Ruling Class* and *Red Noses,* has presented many of the forgotten plays from Shakespeare's time by Ben Jonson and others both on the radio and in Regents Park Theatre. He described realism as a side street which was a dead end for drama.

All of this brings us up to Lance Tait. His plays in this volume demonstrate his belief in the excitement of non-realistic theatre. Strindberg's *Miss Julie* was hailed as a masterpiece of Naturalism when it was first written. Tait has taken the main themes and created a version incorporating fantasy and dreamlike scenes. An engrossing aura is created through the use of taped voices that speak and sing, commenting on the action, foreshadowing and intensifying it. The play is a combination of poetry and prose with much of the poetry spoken by a chorus, harking back to the great dramas of Ancient Greece. In the original play, Miss Julie succumbs to guilt and hypnotic suggestion and cuts her throat with Jean's razor at the end of the play. Tait presents a new and modern take to the ending with a failed suicide attempt. Even as her body lies outside, Miss Julie appears and comments on that fact and the fact that "We live in an age now where more Julies are likely to survive." The fresh look at a familiar play provides a comment on our contemporary society.

The Babysitter provides another example of the breadth of imagination that produces Tait's plays. He begins with directions for the actors that should help to convey the non-realistic "toxic environment." The play starts on familiar ground: a couple sit in a condominium bickering. But immediately, we see that the situation is removed from the familiar: sticking up through the floor of the condo is a fragment of a mangled barbecue. As Stettbacher tries to clean up the mess of grit and sausage residue, he and his wife quarrel about the open window and we perceive that there is something strange about him and their relationship. Into this disturbing scene comes a babysitter. However, her arrival is mysterious as Stettbacher and Debbie have no children. At first they try to get rid of her, then she becomes involved in a nightmare of activity in which the deranged behavior of both husband and wife surround and entrap her. Far from being depressing, the play has a great deal of comedy. The playwright uses music effectively, particularly in the conclusion where the action builds to a startling climax. This is a representation of modern society and modern marriage, but not the usual realistic representation seen so often in the theatre.

In *Germany*, played immediately after *The Babysitter*, Tait takes the action to another strange level. The theme of revenge by a family member on a husband who has caused his wife's death has become familiar through plays, films, and television. Tait creates a new and unconventional set of characters to be played by the same actors who were in *The Babysitter*. The use of lighting and music again creates an alarming and engrossing mood. The character Ilse sets up the action with her first speech, in poetry, against a background of music. Her quest for revenge has led her to track down her ex-brother-in-law Rudi. The situation is one we can see in the newspapers: the husband has caused the wife's death and now has custody of their son. Ilse achieves revenge by shooting him:

One, two, three,
Biddy-bum, biddy-boom, biddy-dee.
He falls, he dies.

But the playwright has another surprise in store as the characters roll the cameras on the action once more, but with a twist.

In *East Play*, Tait makes use of a setting which is simultaneously two quite different places: "An Eastside Manhattan apartment and at the same time a prison cell in the Chinese Laogai." The playwright uses the setting as a means of teaching the audience about Chinese prison camps and about the extension of business into everyday life in our society. The dialogue is interactive between the "terribly rich" person, Carol—and those she dominates—and the Prisoner who protested violations of human rights in Tienanmen Square. The discussions involve the many businesses with which the characters are involved such as "Unsaved Enterprises," "Spit in My Face Branch Offices," and "Penniless Productions." Carol offers to buy the son of a woman who has come to visit, rebukes her butler, Jake, and kicks and beats the Prisoner. The language ranges from realistic, to farcical, and to poetic. The mixture of comedy and poignancy leads to a strong conclusion in which the Prisoner relates the events in Tianmen Square:

> They gutted the camp in the square.
> We ran from that place,
> Leaving the opera of youth
> Stifled under the groaning sky.

This short play offers interesting opportunities for actors and makes its points with wit and irony.

David Mamet Fan Club takes on a provocative subject—the merit of playwright David Mamet. In this play a dialogue is played out between a girl who is tired of the playwright and her boyfriend who nearly worships the playwright. The girl does not believe he has a way with words, "The more Mamet I see, the more I believe he's a fraud." In contrast, Jerry believes that, "David Mamet is greater than the Disney Company." While the piece is apparently an amusing argument about the merits of a particular playwright, in fact it is a reflection on the whole of modern realistic playwriting. Jerry speaks for plays with violent, obscene language and utterly realistic characters intended to be acted by Stanislavskian actors. The Girlfriend quotes Walt Whitman and yearns for a wider approach to art and theatre.

Tait's movement away from realism allows him to incorporate poetry, music, dance, choral work, spectacle, and bizarre characterization in a mixture that not only draws in an audience, but gives the audience an artistic experience that moves beyond that of sheer realism. Later in this volume, Frank Hoff, an expert on Japanese Theater, will speak briefly to some of the playwright's formal and aesthetic influences in his introductory remarks to the last three plays.

Yvonne Shafer
St. John's University
New York

Author's Preface

Realism is a nice business in the theater. Acting students pay millions each year to be instructed how to painstakingly but somehow naturally play realistic stage scenes so truth, or rather The Truth, is manifested. Writers actually have a chance of earning money if they write plays with instant dramatic "payoffs" that grab the spectator with simple characters and easily recognizable situations. (Hopefully this will be done with a small cast around a stage sofa-set for two acts.) It seems that almost anybody can write a play provided only that they put real life under the stage lights. The gratifying presence of the synthetic in art has been nearly hammered into oblivion by the blunt tools of realism and commerce—or so it seems to me on a gray day. Real life reiterated shall never be enough for the artist that wants to make art.

Realism does have its place in all art. How can we appreciate the proper use of realism in the theater? One should read and see plays of other times and places; these plays will indulge the realistic, the better ones not to the exclusion of symbol, poetry, fantasy, etc. Such plays will be far richer than our "straight plays". (Incidentally, the only type of non-realistic theater that Americans have gotten good at is the musical; but there is a problem with the musical still being stuck in the 1950s, despite of "The Lion King", "Rent", "Hair" and the presence of the British composer Andrew Lloyd Webber.)

I think some theater practitioners find it hard to read plays of the past, and plays of other cultures partly because they have the mistaken idea that knowledge gained from literature is of little use to their "cutting edge" *now* approach, in other words, their *realistic* approach. Of course, art cannot be truly real, its power lies in the fact that it is glorious fakery. Too often those who advocate realistic drama-making are offering pat answers to the difficulties of telling a story. I want to tell these people that detail is no substitute for depth. And depth is not the winning of predictable responses from the audience, moment by moment throughout an entire piece of theater. Whoever is wont to manufacture all the responses in an audience treats their audience like machines.

Among other things, I believe a play must have variety and a vital density. Entrenching ourselves in realism invites trouble—I should say boredom. We all are attracted to the beautiful, the elaborated, the dramatic, etc.—these may exist for us in mundane life, but for a number of reasons they might not be any fun. I expect *life* to be *played with* in art. Art that is produced according to Naturalism comes up short; when one is being stubbornly realistic one betrays the whole concept of what art is.

Audiences need to share in the act of theater. Theater pieces saturated with realism seem to me to sit up on stage in some sort of large fishbowl. Such a set-up incites a voyeuristic, sidelining experience in people—especially if the actors provoke merely empathy within me for their characters. Koestler, in *The Ghost in the Machine*, calls attention the perils of identification and the arousal of vicarious emotions; he notes that political rallies, voodoo sessions, etc. can also help us to transcend ourselves and forget about our worries; and energized identification is able incite us to the actions of a mob. In good theater, the spectator ought to *wonder*, he or she must experience a freeing integration with the theater work, a reaction that ultimately promotes health, not destruction; post-performance the spectator will have a dialogue within him- or herself over the meanings in the play, meanings that often go beyond the matters of character, or one sole feature of the drama.

We need to see more than escalating psychological conflicts (with a public outrage thrown in) that only modestly comment upon our condition as human beings. Inadequately-grounded teachers, slaves to pseudo-scientific thinking in the arts, are partly to blame for passing down the biases in favor of run-away realism. I can only say that the statement/restatement of the commonplace found over and over again in plays that have "street credibility" supplies us with "little truths". In our own development, our greater truths are not for the most part revealed to us by hitting us immediately squarely in the face. So too it is with drama: a person needs to find his or her own way through ideas before gaining in understanding. It is not theater's job to do all the thinking for us; and if theater rides roughshod over the way we think then we should certainly talk back at it.

Though we live in the Age of Science and now, the so-called Information Age as well, we must not completely surrender ourselves to "getting real". We must fight the era's urge to make art a rational endeavor, to make art brim with street-real data to the exclusion of penetrating, evocative images. As a species, our hunger for different perspectives, for the otherworldly and the fantastic, and our thirst for the spiritual/metaphysical dimension have not been bled or bred out of us. Such needs and instincts cannot be exercised fully in an encounter with a pedestrian art that tries to be the perfectly right thing because it is some sort of Real Thing.

Miss Julie

after August Strindberg

This is not a literal translation but a radical reworking of *Miss Julie*, the Strindberg classic of Naturalism. There is less haranguing, hand-wringing and realistic repartee between the characters in my play compared to the Strindberg work. Contemporary dance is a significant feature in this new *Miss Julie*. The action of the play is set in the southern United States.

I have retained much of the original *Miss Julie* story. I have stripped the Strindberg characters down to their meaningful skins and reclothed them as I have seen fit. My reconfiguration of this play has been influenced by various 19th century materials; it is also influenced by the post-*Julie* life and works of Strindberg; furthermore, the struggles of Stanislaw Witkiewicz to break with the confines of realistic drama has influenced me; lastly, of course, my own experience of life and of theater shows through in the play.

In this play, and the other plays in this book, I look for presentational acting, as opposed to representational acting styles.

This play was initiated thanks to Bruce McIntosh and Lisa Rhoden. A reading of this play, directed by Don Elwell, was presented by Greylight Theatre in Murphysboro, Illinois on August 20, 1999.

The Characters

Miss Julie	Female, 28 years old.
Jean	Male, 33 years old.
Christine	Female, 35 years old.
Dancer #1/Kevin	Male.
Dancer #2/Dan	Male.
Dancer #3/Mia/ the Dad	Female.
Last Dancer/Louise	Female.
The Chorus	Comprised of the four Dancers.

Place: The southern United States, not far from the Gulf of Mexico, in the kitchen of the main house on a large farm.

Time: The end of the twentieth century.

Miss Julie

The Scene

A large farm in the southern United States near the Gulf of Mexico. Inside the kitchen of the main house.

Lights up on Miss Julie. *Most of the set remains in the dark. Before the music begins we hear the sound of many birds. Slow music fades in, the sound of the birds fades out.* Miss Julie *moves in slow motion to the slow music. Her movements begin to make sense: she is dancing with an invisible dance partner*

Popular dance music interrupts. At once a group of Dancers *(including the* Last Dancer*) enters in step with the music. The* Dancers *come together: the formation that they create looks something like tree.* Miss Julie *stops and watches them. The voices on tape begin.*

Voices: *(On tape):*
   The short Midsummer Eve,
   The unequal partners,
   Hear vertigo,

During the next words, Miss Julie *begins to dance. She has a superior look about her.*

Voices: *(On tape.)*
   Know that she's the last of the line,
   That she can't be bullied—

Miss Julie *walks out. The* Dancers *move, disentwining themselves; they take less than a minute. Then they exit, dancing, except the* Last Dancer. *The music ends abruptly.*

Last Dancer: The dance of Midsummer's Eve. (*She gestures to where the dancers have just exited.*) Here, inside. A large kitchen of a country estate.

New music begins and the Last Dancer *exits.* Jean *and* Christine *enter to the music, he carrying a table, she a chair. Lights up on the whole set: there is a strange openness to this "kitchen". Abstract design tendencies prevail—despite the presence of a sink, a counter, a cupboard and a stove. The music ends;* Jean *and* Christine *place the table and chair down.*

Jean: Miss Julie was with the fields manager. Soon as she sees me, she rushes over and offers her hand. I didn't say no. We danced. She was possessed. By what, I don't know.

Christine: She's upset still. From her break-up. With Roberts.

Jean: Very little modesty with that one.

Christine: Which one? Roberts?

Jean: I saw them. In the stables. She made him leap over her whip. Like you teach a dog a trick. He jumped twice. Each time after, she rewarded him with a piece of food. The third time he grabbed the whip and held its handle to her throat. He threw it down and stamped out. That's the last we saw of Clem Roberts.

Different music starts.

Jean:
There's closeness, shirts cling to wet flesh.
A sweet friction...

Christine: *(Not hearing him.)* I saved some supper for you. *(He goes over to the counter and touches the plate of food.)*

Jean: The plate's not warmed.

Christine: You are fussy, aren't you?

Jean *picks up the plate, finds a fork, goes to the table and sits down to eat. He says grace:*

Jean:
O Earth and far-shining Sun,
Please sustain us,
Especially the lost souls among us,
Show them the path to your grace.

Christine *is pleasantly taken by surprise by Jean's act of prayer.*

Christine: *(Smiling.)* What a surprise. *(She reaches over and plays with his hair.)*

Jean: Please don't do that, Christine. You know I don't like it.

Christine: 'Loving you, Jean—

Jean *eats a biteful, then:*

Jean: I've taken Miss Julie's father down to the coast.

Christine *smiles, goes over to the counter drawer and pulls out a bottle of beer. She holds it for his approval.*

Jean: No. I want wine.

Christine: Wine?

Jean: It's Midsummer's Eve. *(He rises from the table. He goes to the cupboard where has hidden some wine and a takes out a bottle.)* Here. *(Defensively.)* They can spare it.

He opens the bottle and sets it on the table. Christine *brings him a wine glass. He holds up the empty glass and looks into the "bell" of the wine glass. He pours the wine into the glass. He tastes the wine.*

Jean: Ah, the old man knows his wines.

Christine: You seem to know yourself, too.

Jean: I may, I may.

Christine: Will you dance with me tonight?

Jean: Of course.

Christine: Promise?

Jean: Yes.

Miss Julie *comes in from the dance. She shouts back to others at the dance as she enters the kitchen:*

Miss Julie: Go on without me. (Jean *rises from the table, and drinks up the wine in the glass. He gives the glass and the wine bottle to* Christine. *She puts the bottle away.* Miss Julie *still shouts to someone at the dance.)* I shall return. *(At Miss Julie's entrance, Jean rises from the table. She addresses him and* Christine.) What's wrong? We're all having a fantastic time. Why stay in here?

Jean: Maybe your father will be needing a ride back from the coast.

Miss Julie: How very conscientious of you.

Jean: Excuse me, Miss. (Jean *wipes his mouth on a napkin and starts to leave.*)

Miss Julie: Where are you going, Jean? (*A command.*) Slower. (*She conducts him back to near the table.*) Come. (*She stops where she wants him.*)

Jean: If it's part of my job, I'll stay.

Miss Julie: I am different from most people. I'm sure I have my mother to blame for that. She was a sort of all-rounder. She would not look down upon this, tonight. She respected *pleasure.* Christine, you don't mind if I ask Jean to dance with me once more—

Christine: If you want to dance with him, he'll do it.

Miss Julie: Oh, for God's sake!

Jean: Miss Julie, I just danced with you. It'll look unusual for us to dance again so soon. You know the way people talk.

Miss Julie: Let them talk. I'm the lady of the house. I honor the help by choosing one of them to dance with me. *You* know how to partner a lady.

Jean: I am at your service.

Miss Julie: I'm not ordering you. We're all just folks enjoying ourselves. There's nobody too good to dance with anybody else—as long as they can dance well. It's a special time—the short night is a great equalizer. (*To* Jean.) Give me your hand.

He gives her his hand and she walks him out. Christine *is alone in the kitchen. Dance music starts.* Christine *tidies up after* Jean. *Then, while the music is still playing, two female* Dancers (Dancer #3 *and the* Last Dancer) *enter, dancing to the music, from the rear of the stage. They "dance at"*

Christine *but she does little more than sway to the music.* Voices *on tape are heard:*

Female Voices: *(On tape.)*
> To fly, to glide, to soar,
> You've felt like this before.

The two female Dancers *exit and the music number ends.* Jean *comes in alone from the dance.*

Jean: Everyone was pretending not to look. Miss Julie needs to dance. It'll kill her or cure her. I hope you're all right. *(Pause.* Christine *nods, "yes".)*

Christine: There'd be no use in me saying no.

Miss Julie *enters.*

Miss Julie: *(Seeing* Jean.) There you are! You're a fine gentleman, running off from your partner like that.

Jean: On the contrary, Miss Julie, I was returning to my partner. I promised Christine I'd dance with her.

Miss Julie: *(To* Christine.) Jean seems more than on a friendly basis with you.

Christine: You've been engaged yourself.

Miss Julie: So it's gone that far? I hadn't heard. I wish you success. *(Pause.)* Jean, you're not dressed properly.

Jean: For what?

Miss Julie: This isn't work. Run upstairs to my father's room. Find one of his shirts.

Jean: I can wear my own shirts, thank you.

Jean *leaves quickly.*

Miss Julie: Jean is a quick and clever man. He's not long for here, I'm afraid. He's been to too many other places to stay. *(Long pause. They listen to the music.)* We wouldn't want to lose him, would we?—

Christine: It's getting late, Miss.

Pause. They wait for Jean.

Miss Julie: He'll be wanting his freedom at some point. It's rather a cruel joke that a man with so much of what it takes to get ahead sets his sights so low. Let's not care tonight, though. We abandon all concerns. (Jean *enters.)* Oh, where have you been? *(Apologizing.)* It's rude of me to ask. *(Pause.)* Let's let out that shirt of yours. I don't know how you manage. *(She untucks his shirt some.)* That still won't do. Christine, go to my father's oak wardrobe. Bring me that light blue shirt he keeps there.

Pause. Christine *leaves to get the shirt. Another pause.* Miss Julie *walks around* Jean *and looks him up and down.*

Miss Julie: Have you ever been out near the pond at night?

Jean: I suppose.

Miss Julie: Because *I* was out there one night. A beautiful, starry night. A man was taking a woman from behind. You were not that man, were you?

Jean: Miss Julie has colorful imagination.

Miss Julie: No, I saw it.

Jean: Begging your pardon, Miss, but it would be best to change the subject.

Miss Julie: The subject is as old as the hills.

Jean: That it is, ma'am.

Miss Julie: You shouldn't be riled by something that's been going on for so long, Jean. Please, sit down.

Jean: All right.

Jean *sits down.*

Miss Julie: Why do you resist me?

Jean: I'm sitting down, Miss. *(Pause. She stares at him.)* I respect your father.

Miss Julie: So do I.

Jean: He is my employer.

Miss Julie: Oh, now that you're sitting down, I'm afraid I have to ask you to get me a drink.

Jean: *(Getting up.)* What would you like?

Miss Julie: My tastes are simple. Beer.

Jean *(To himself.)* Last of the line.

Jean *goes to the cupboard and gets a bottle of beer. He opens it and pours it into a glass.*

Miss Julie: Pour yourself some too. A lady isn't allowed to drink alone.

Jean *pours himself a small glass of beer.*

Jean *(To himself again.)*
    Herding his sheep on the high hill,
    The shepherd encounters a lost maid.

Miss Julie: What's that you say?

Jean *brings the two glasses of beer and sets them on the table.*

Jean: Something as old as the hills.

Miss Julie *gestures for him to sit down. He sits down.*

Miss Julie: So we both have a sense of history. Now, drink a toast to me.

He briefly tilts his head in a respectful gesture and raises his glass politely.

Jean: To the lady of the house.

Miss Julie: *(Smiles, then:)* And to history. Now, to complete our toast, kiss my foot, please. (Jean *looks at her incredulously.)* My foot. Kiss it. It's part of the old gallant's ceremony.

Jean *quickly thinks his way out of the situation.*

Jean: To kiss the *glove.*

Miss Julie: I'm wearing no gloves. My foot will have to do. But if you're not man enough to do it— *(He looks at her. He listens to hear if* Christine *is approaching. He boldly grabs Miss Julie's calf and kisses her foot.)* Excellent. (Jean *puts down her leg.)*

Jean: How much do you want people talking about you?

Miss Julie: Oh, you just broke the spell. Why must you constantly watch your back? (Christine *enters with the father's blue shirt.)* There we are. Put it on, Jean. (Jean *takes the shirt from* Christine. *He goes into a corner of the room, turns his back to the women, and changes into it.* Miss Julie *comments on his modesty.)* How very quaint. (Jean *comes* *back with his own shirt in hand and puts it on the counter top.)* Now the picture's painted. (Christine *fusses over* Jean *in the new shirt.)*

Christine: *(To* Jean, *quietly.)* Don't let her make you do anything you don't want to do.

Miss Julie: What was that?

Christine: I'm telling him I'll clean the shirt in the morning.

Miss Julie: You people think of everything.

Christine: *(To* Jean *only.)* I'm going to bed. I know when there isn't a chance.

Miss Julie: The shirt looks perfect on him. *(Pause. To* Christine.) You're going to bed?

Christine: Yes. Just making arrangements for tomorrow. Goodnight. *(She exits.)*

Miss Julie: Come outside with me.

Jean: I don't think so.

Miss Julie: Someone might see us and talk.

Jean: Yes. They'll say you lowered yourself.

Miss Julie: Maybe the way that's cut out for me is too high. *(She feigns losing her balance, then feigns falling. She laughs.)*

Jean: You're strange.

Miss Julie:
　　I am—perhaps you are too.
　　It's all strange.
　　We're part of the swamp, Jean,

Where seed sticks to scum and they float
Down the stream, merrily, merrily,
Life is but a hope,
Fallen against a dream.

She laughs.

Jean, you and I—come on—

(She motions to the outdoors with a toss of her head.) Under the stars. Whatever worries us, whatever vexations we may have will be put to rest by the night. *(Pause.)* You don't have the... strength?

Jean: That's not it, Miss Julie.

Miss Julie:
I dream that I climb out of the black water
And up a hill on jagged stairs—
Someone has given me medicine
To calm me down but I can't find peace.

Jean: Go to bed, Julie.

Miss Julie: I want to fly, but all I do is hang in the air.

Jean: *(Pause.)* Fine things to be talking about.

Miss Julie: I must force you to go outside with me. You don't want me to pester anyone else with such odd talk, do you?

She gives him her arm. Jean *is torn over whether to go outside. He takes her arm. They start to go out. Suddenly he puts a hand to one of his eyes.*

Jean: Excuse me. *(He stops.)*

Miss Julie: Have you got something in your eye?

Jean: Yes.

Miss Julie: What could it be? Sit down. I'll get it out. *(She leads him over to the chair and sits him down. She makes him tilt his head back.)* There. *(She gently holds part of Jean's eyelid.)* I'll have to pull it a little. To move whatever it is to the corner. (Jean *is restless.)* Sit still. *(She slaps his hand. Pause)* You're nervous! *(She feels his biceps.)* My, what strong arms.

Jean: None of that, Miss Julie.

Miss Julie: Sit. *(She moves the bit of dust to the corner of his eye.)* There. It must be gone. Kiss my hand, please.

Jean: What?

Miss Julie: To thank me.

Jean *gets up from the chair.*

Jean: Now, listen. Christine's gone.

Miss Julie: Indeed.

Jean: Listen to me or else.

Miss Julie: Kiss my hand first.

Jean: Or else—

Miss Julie: Kiss my hand.

Jean: You have only yourself to blame—

She extends her hand. Jean kisses it. He then grabs her waist and pulls her to him and kisses her on the mouth. She resists the kiss.

Miss Julie: Stop it.

Voices: *(On tape.)*
Last of the line,
Know that she can't be bullied—

Jean: You're toying with me, ma'am.

Miss Julie: There's nothing wrong. *(She refers to the kitchen.)* Except just not here. We were about to go outside.

Jean: *(Pause.)* Maybe you like to be *seen*.

Miss Julie: I prefer privacy.

Another piece of dance music plays beyond the doors of the kitchen. With these words she fondles him "absently".

Jean: You do? *(Tired of the "game".)* If you don't mind, I'll get back to my work.

Miss Julie: There's no work. The pond awaits us. You have one horn. *(She makes a gesture to his crotch.)* You can be my unicorn. *(She laughs.)* We'll beat the grass down.

Jean: Excuse me?

Miss Julie: The virgin is put out in the clearing. Where they know the unicorn's path passes through. The unicorn comes into the meadow, smells her, shifts his eyes this way and that, then leaps into her lap—she gives him her milk.

Jean: The funny things you say.

Miss Julie: And the unicorn gets drunk on that milk.

Jean: You're the one who's already drunk.

Miss Julie: Just like my dad, the man you are so respectful of. But I hold it better than he does, don't you agree? I'll go down in family history for that sole fact. If anyone should care.

Pause.

Jean: Yeah, who cares?

Miss Julie: *(Surprised by the remark.)* That's not being sociable. *(Pause. She changes her tone.)* You must pay the penalty for being rude to me. *(She looks glances around the room once.)* I would strike you with a whip for that. But there isn't one. You must make amends. I'm going to ask you a question. A serious one, of a personal nature. Answer me the truth—otherwise you shall never be forgiven. And to live unforgiven by me is terrible. *(Pause.)* Have you ever been in love, Jean?

Jean: "We're all just folks enjoying ourselves."—you're as nosy as anybody.

Miss Julie: Oh, Jean, careful. ...Have you?

Jean: You won't remember a thing tomorrow, so I don't mind.

Years ago when my father still worked, I'd come over with him when he made his evening rounds. I didn't always get out of the truck. Especially when there was a little girl playing in the yard. *(He smiles at the thought of summer.)* That would make it summer, because she was finally home from boarding school.

I wanted to play with her but my parents always said no, we were not of the same class.

Miss Julie: So you could only sit and watch me?

Jean: Yes.

Miss Julie: And eventually *you* went away.

Jean: A young man has other dreams. More attainable, perhaps.

Miss Julie: Tell me more—

Jean: I've already answered your one big serious question so you can forgive me and I can live spared from your fury.

Miss Julie: Very sarcastic. *(She shakes her head in disapproval.)*

Jean: I expected by now that you'd be married. To some rich man. *(Pause.)* At least I don't have to get my britches all twisted up because I'm in line to inherit a fortune.

Miss Julie: Thankfully no such future is in store for you.

Jean: Some people say that things can change, though.

Miss Julie: Yes, but in what way? Maybe only in the way my father says: "The ice shelves of the Western Antarctic are slowly collapsing. Before long, the level of the sea will rise and bury the great cities of the coast; then our farm'll be run by bugs and snakes."

But where were we? How fast the human mind veers into the complicated and ridiculous. *(Pause.)* I know. Get the key to the boathouse. Row me out on the pond. I want to see the sunrise.

Jean: Sunrise? No. I'll need to be ready to pick up your father.

Miss Julie: But you're so responsible.

Jean: I would like to keep my job.

Miss Julie: You will. Let Daddy have his few drinks down at the coast before it washes away. He won't need you in the morning.

Jean: He might care about what I'm getting up to with you.

Miss Julie: His mind is busy with other matters entirely.

Jean: What about Christine?

Miss Julie: Put your hand here. *(She takes his hand and places it just below her navel. The dance music in the next room starts to fade.)* That's a start. *(The music ends.)* You must help the starling spread her little wings. And fly off into ecstasy.

Jean: The music's ended. *(He hears footsteps.)* Somebody's coming. I'd rather not have them find us here together.

The Chorus *enters almost effortlessly.*

Chorus:
Why do we come into the kitchen?
Are we here to satisfy our appetites?

They look accusingly at her.

We've had our appetites displayed as long as
History has been sung.
Let's relate some history:

To Miss Julie:

Everyday your mother realized it was too late,
She knew she was going to have a baby
By a man who loved the grape.
Many times she cried
While he raised the glass with friends
Down at the red horizon.
When they got married her family was calmed
By his bountiful rice fields,
And his bicentennial name.
But how to endure in that salt-bit-up air?
—He always hid under the brim of a hat,
Reaching for gin, to douse the fire in his brain.

She did not notice her slip into despair:
There was that babe between 'em—
That worked as a diversion for a while.

Miss Julie: Why aren't you dancing?

Chorus:
We're not happy, dancing have-nots
Like in some opera created for the haves.
We've been drinking
And we feel like saying what's on our minds.

Miss Julie: Yes, you're drunk and you come to abuse me.

Chorus:
Enough of history; here's simply a story:
The princess of the local estuary
Sits on the muddy banks, casting her eyes o'er the
        water.
He paddles through on a raft
And what should come from *her* lips
But a siren song, flashing like a silver fish in the sun!
How it draws him to her,
How like a strong smell it envelopes him,
As he gets closer,
How his freedom is abridged,
His hands go limp,
Her face, oh, softly guides his neck into
        her guillotine,
He thinks he some how's touching feathery wings.
But the blade slices his head off.

Miss Julie: You're jealous of me. You're jealous that Jean's enjoying my company! I'm sorry you feel this way. Remember that for years I was a child among the rest of you children here.

Chorus: You want tonight's summer dish. *(The dish they allude to is* Jean.*)*

> He's one of us.
> It isn't right that you demand anything from us
>   this night
> Tonight is the earth's night, it's for the
>   common things.
> You're trying to ring a bell over us,
> We're not listening, master,
> We can't hear the call.
>
> But *he* does, maybe he's got the notion
> That he's better than us.
> It will come to pass
> That you shall have every inch of his body.

They laugh.

Miss Julie: They're horrible *birds*, mocking me. *(The* Chorus *exits.)* How quickly they forget what's been done for them. I'll lock them out.

Jean: No. You can't.

Miss Julie:

> I wonder how easy they would find it
> To be born into what I have.
>
> I will not be called an enticer,
> By those who let loose their crazy voices
> For their perverse delight.
> We have a farm to run,
> Many mouths to feed.
> The conditions here are good—
>
> They shall be punished.
> Monday they'll pull on their boots,
> Go out into edges of the farm,
> Where the mosquitoes are bloated

And the land's soaked to a hazard;
There they'll work
To mend fence.

Jean:
The fences don't need to be fixed.
There're no cattle out there.

Miss Julie:
It's their punishment, Jean.
Awful work for awful people.

Jean: You know they're drunk. (*He tries to calm her.*) Come over to the window. (*They face the audience and look out an imaginary window. Pause. He points.*) You see that?

Miss Julie: A deer?

Jean: No. (*With good humor.*) Bats. (Jean *laughs.*) *She does not find it funny.*)

Miss Julie: This farm has been fair to its help.

Jean: The deer eat well, they're strong enough to protect themselves from the fox. (*She relaxes a little and touches* Jean *on his chest. He moves carefully away a few inches. Beyond the room, a new piece of dance music begins.*) Where are we moving to—pleasure, or pain? (*He takes hold of her arms, brings her to him. He kisses her. This time she does not pull away.*)

Miss Julie: Yes.

Jean: Let's go up to my room.

Miss Julie: Oh, you're giving the orders now.

Jean: You don't like that? (*She breaks away from him.*)

Miss Julie: What if I don't want to do it in a servant's room?

Jean: Do what? You mean *fuck*? We talk any longer and we won't get to fuck. A man gets tired, Miss Julie. You sure are a lot of work.

Miss Julie: You want to take me up to your room so you can boast that you had the old man's daughter right under his nose?

Jean: He's not home.

Miss Julie: Oh, you're vile. Christine! I need you. Where are you? *(He laughs. She calls.)* Christine!

Jean: She's gone to bed.

Miss Julie: Don't be an animal to me.

Jean: Settle down, Julie. *(Again, she does not notice that he has called her "Julie.")*

Miss Julie: I thought I could trust you because you've been *around*. On your own. Why did you come back when you could have stayed away?

Jean: I like to think I was following my instincts.

Miss Julie: Well, I'm glad you did.

He kisses her tenderly.

Jean: A lady like you shouldn't tease. You'll leave a man hanging.

Miss Julie: I won't—

The dance music ends.

Jean: The dance is over.

Miss Julie: Jean, let's go. Now. Up to your room.

They exit to Jean's room.

Pantomime: the Four Dancers *enter, they are:* Dan, Louise, Kevin *and* Mia; Dan *and* Mia *are noticeably drunk. Slow music, that is, music that does not call attention to its pulse, is heard.*

Dan *comes in with* Louise, Dan *sashays around like a rich man who expects to be waited on hand and foot.* Kevin *and* Mia *watch.* Dan *sits down and puts out his hand for a manicure from* Louise. *She thinks he just wants his hand kissed, so she kisses it.* Dan *wants the manicure. She refuses him. He scolds her.* Louise *gestures to him: first he will want a manicure, then he'll want a massage.* Dan *agrees.* Louise *then gestures that after the massage,* Dan *will want sex. She is not willing to do that. The slow music stops.* Louise *speaks:*

Louise: What do you think I am, a whore?

Kevin *and* Mia *laugh. The pantomime is over.*

Mia: Where's Miss Julie?

Dan: Wouldn't you like to know?

Louise: Busy with Jean, I bet.

Dan: All that dancing is a bad imitation of what's supposed to be done lying down.

Kevin: Anyway, they're in bed now.

Mia: What are they supposed to do, *screw* on the dance floor?

Louise: *(Sarcastically.)* They're not screwing. He's giving her a hundred tiny hair brush strokes before she turns out the light and they go sleepy-sleepy in his bed. *(Pause.)* Let's have some coffee.

Dan: I'm too drunk.

Louise: Go to bed, then.

Dan: If I do, the room'll start spinning 'round. Then I can't sleep. I don't want to sleep. Don't get me wrong. I'd like to go to bed with you all. Except him. *(He means Kevin.)* I should stay awake. Or I'm dead.

Louise: We wouldn't want that.

Mia: Kevin, tell him a story. Help him stay awake.

Kevin: Miss Julie may think she's the only educated person around.

Mia: Tell him one that the princess told. She needed to keep the sheik awake or she would be put to death. Dan, do you really think you're going to die?

Dan: I hope not soon.

Mia: Kevin, tell him. Save his drunken life.

Kevin: In the evil kingdom, it was King Shahriar's habit to force a princess to marry him and then kill her the next day. You see, King Shahriar had a thing for unspoiled women. He couldn't abide by anything but virgins. Times were different in those days.

Dan *and* Mia *laugh.*

Mia: The evil bastard never got laid good.

Kevin: There was a clever princess—her name was Sheherazade.

Like the other young brides she had no choice, she was forced to marry King Shahriar. And on the account of her inexperience in sex, there was no way she was going to turn things in her favor that way.

She used her tongue the only way she knew how: she told stories. It was her plan to go on and on till sunrise. Then the sheik would be worn out and he'd forget about doing anything to her. Oh—she never got to the punch line in her stories before the sheik went to sleep. That way, he had to keep her alive through the next day. And that next day she'd start a whole new story with a incomplete end.

After one thousand and one nights the king withdrew the threat of death upon her and they lived happily ever after.

Mia: But still he had evil lurking inside.

Dan: And the moral of the story is we'll never learn if she ever tried to get good in bed. But she sure had the gift to gab. Tell me another story. How about one concerning our Miss Julie?

Mia: She had that boyfriend, Roberts.

Dan: No, before that. Way before that. Her first guy, The guy that turned up here. (*To* Louise.) You tell it. I'm in the mood for love.

Louise: No.

Dan: Why won't you tell it?

Louise: Because I'm not as drunk as you.

Dan: We saw them. She stopped playing the piano when he walked in. She had a thin bathrobe on—silk. *Henry* was visiting, they put him up in the guest room, but now they were in the parlor.

She kept close to the piano, though she got up off the bench. She chattered and they laughed. Henry leaned over, his fingers lightly touched her as they continued to speak. Louise, you were looking too. He put his fingers into her robe.

All the while they were talking about music and lofty subjects, playing innocent, with his hand on her. They moved nearer to the sofa, once there, she broke away and showed him some things—stunts she had learned in gym class in boarding school. Every time she did, her robe flew open and her chest showed.

Okay. Jump forward, ten minutes or so—she said that they shouldn't do it. But he stroked and they kissed, she finally gave in. I think it was her idea to straddle him.

Louise: *(Sarcastically.)* That was very nice, thank you.

Dan: After they stopped she had a weeping fit. We heard her say she didn't think he loved her.

Louise: All right, that's enough.

Dan: You're such a prude.

Louise: No, I believe in a person's privacy.

Dan: You didn't then.

Louise: I was wrong. I'm going to bed.

Dan: What a spoil-sport.

Kevin: I'm going to bed too.

Mia: Me too.

Dan: *(To* Mia.) Alone, my darling?

Mia: *(Sarcastically.)* No, I thought I'd sleep with my brother.

Dan: That's what I've thought all along.

Kevin: Good night, Dan. (Kevin, Louise *and* Mia *exit.)*

Dan: I guess I better go too.

Dan *exits. The stage is empty. Pause. A recording of second part of Margherita's aria, "L'altra notte in fondo al mare", from Arrigo Boito's opera,* Mefistofele, *begins. The recording shall last two minutes and few seconds.*

Miss Julie *enters slowly during the aria. She would be sleeping next to* Jean, *except we need her on stage in order to glimpse her state of mind. The music and singing of the aria are important for establishing atmosphere; the words of the second part of the aria do not always literally connect to the play's action; for reference, the words, and their translation are:)*

In letargico sopore	(My mother is put to rest
è mia madre addormentata,	in a deep death-sleep,
e per colmo dell'orrore	and to crown the horror
dicon ch'io l'abbia attoscata.	they say I poisoned her.
L'aura è fredda, il carcere fosco,	The night is cold, the prison, black,
e la mesta anima mia,	and my miserable soul,
come il passero del bosco,	like a sparrow of the wood,
vola, vola, vola... via.	flies, flies, flies off...
Ah! pietà di me!	Ah! have mercy on me!)

Miss Julie *can be seen by the audience as early as the words, "è mia madre" when she enters with a few steps. Her appearance is ghostly. At the words, "L'aura è fredda" she looks around, tormented. She takes a deep breath by the words "anima mia". During the remainder of the aria she is in a state of distress. She only takes a few steps across the stage, sometimes looking out into the distance. She always proceeds slowly—making sure the audience can study her. At the final measures of the aria, with the words, "pietà di me!", she looks down to the ground. Her head is half-bowed by the close of the aria. She pauses. Then the music ends.*

Miss Julie:
The man beside me sleeps,
His shoulder is slung over the side of the bed.
No matter what he intends,
I intend to have him do as I say.
He'll go down the path I choose
To my music, to my breath.

She laughs.

If a man can be touched by a woman
Then he is overcome.

Pause.

I'm tormented, Jean,
Winged things peck at my flesh,
A flexing cormorant screeches.

Miss Julie, *with the* **Chorus:** (The Chorus *is off stage.*)
The pain must be dulled.

Miss Julie: *(Alone.)*
I'm drowning,
I need to reach the top for air.

The sound of wind is heard.

But once there, I'm suffocated
By the ripping... wind,
There's no way out, Jean, I've tried—
I want to be a child again,
Tumbling down a grassy hill,
All is flat, my dear,
Except for the roof above.

The wind dies down, but not out. Miss Julie, *child-like-an-animal, prowls around the stage. She sometimes interrupts this with skipping. The next five lines are said in a childish voice:*

Oh, Daddy, away at the blustery sea,
When you going to come home with a kiss for me?
I've got a blossom fixed in my hair,
Would like you like one, too?
Come back. *(With bitter acceptance.)* You don't care.

Mama did, until she started her new life with a man whom I can't stand. There should be some law prohibiting the amount of golf that any featherbrain is allowed to play.

She exits to go back to Jean's room.

Pause. The sound of crickets and frogs. Before too long the sun starts to rise. Sounds of morning—nothing so obvious as a rooster crowing, though. The sun shines obliquely through the window. Light hits the leaves of a tree outside. Jean *comes in from his room.*

Jean: Miss Julie was a wild one last night. Midsummer's Eve dance—they really thought up a good one, when they thought that up.

Rise and shine,
Last of the Line.
She knows her family can't stay
Up high forever.

Christine *enters. She is partly dressed for church.*

Christine: Who are you talking to?

Jean: *(Ignoring the question.)* 'Morning. *(He goes to her and gives her a quick kiss.)* Going to church.

Christine: It's Sunday. *(She has asked the following question many times before, with the same answer.)* You coming with me?

Jean: No, Christine.

Christine: I have to ask—

Jean: I know.

Christine: *(Warmly.)* If I wasn't so tired... seeing that Julie's father is gone... I would have sneaked into your room.

Jean: They'll be other nights.

Christine: How many times did you dance—after I left?

Jean: Once too many. She was not to be refused.

Christine: I don't imagine so. They'll be talking about it for weeks, won't they? That's all you did, right?

Jean: What?

Christine: Dance.

Jean: Yeh. *(He lies.)*

Christine: Jean, I know you had no say in the matter. When she says jump, you have to jump. It shouldn't have to be like that.

Jean: But you'll forgive her?

Christine: I will. The world wasn't made perfect.

Jean: Mm hmm. *(Sarcastically.)* And God tests us. For this world's a poor copy of the greater world to come.

Christine: If you have a problem with going to church, just leave it at that.

Jean: I'm sure I'll be forgiven for my trespasses.

Christine: I don't want to lose you, Jean. Respect my beliefs, please do. It's hard for me to live with the sin of having sex with you. But I love you. Don't make things tougher on me by criticizing my faith.

Jean: I'm sorry we don't always see things the same way.

Christine: Not as sorry as I am. *(Pause.)* Jean, I just always want you to tell me the truth.

Jean: You may be hearing some things you don't want to hear from them.

Christine: Who?

Jean: The others. At the dance. Like, that I slept with Miss Julie afterwards.

Christine: You didn't.

Jean: But I did.

Christine: You bastard.

Jean: I'm telling the truth. It was nothing serious. She was teasing me.

Christine: You were drunk.

Jean: I had a little.

Christine *bursts into tears.*

Christine: Are you trying to punish me?

Jean: No.

Christine: Why'd you do it?

Jean: She had it coming to her.

Christine: Stop it. *(Pause. For a moment she shows control.)* I quit. I've lost all respect for my employers.

Jean: What do they need your respect for?

Christine: It's the way I live, Jean. I suppose your morals, if you have any, are flexible enough for you to be around those you disrespect.

Jean: For given amounts of time. You can't change the way things are.

Christine: People can change, Jean.

Jean: I don't think so, Christine. But let's ease up. I guess we've fulfilled the Christian quota on the seventh day for reflection upon the morals of man—all in lightning speed. Time to get back to the grindstone for me.

Christine: You never talked this way before last night.

Jean: Maybe you never *heard* me before this.

Christine: I've got to get ready for church. *(Sounds of footsteps are heard on the floor above.)* Is that her father? Is he finally back?

Jean: No, it's not the old man.

Christine: Oh, *she's* up there. That's right. I'll go. 'Don't want anybody to feel awkward.

Christine *exits. Pause.* Miss Julie *comes down from Jean's room.*

Miss Julie: There you are. *(She goes to Jean and gives him a brief kiss.)* Oh, I'm feeling a little weak. Like a sparrow who's brushed and bruised her wing. Was that Christine down here? I thought I heard her.

Jean: Yes, it was. How are you?

Miss Julie: If you don't mind me saying, I think you and she are mismatched.

Jean: You do your best with what's around. She's gone now.

Miss Julie: It's one of the drawbacks of the country. Just making do. You need new blood. Or else all wastes away and dies. *(She kisses him once more.)* Tell me, why *did* you move back here?

Jean: I told you. *(Shrugging.)* Anyway, I always felt at home here.

Miss Julie: It's a pleasant feeling?

Jean: I said I feel at home.

Miss Julie: Don't get too cozy. You haven't married the boss's daughter yet.

Jean: *(Ignoring the remark.)* Did you get much sleep?

Miss Julie: I was hoping you'd say you moved back because you loved me and couldn't live without me.

Jean: I didn't know you were going to be here.

Miss Julie: Well, I am. Jean, would you like to go on a trip? To celebrate? Do you feel like traveling when you're with someone and you're happy?

Jean: There's work to do.

Miss Julie: After last night, all you can think of is work?

Jean: It's hard to forget, Miss Julie.

Miss Julie: You can call me *Julie.*

Jean: I did before. Twice. You just didn't notice. Anyway, what would we live on if we just took off from here?

Miss Julie: I'm talking about a vacation! There's always money to be found for a vacation. *(Shyly, sweetly.)* Come, tell me that you love me.

Jean: *(Pause.)* You may think you love me.

Miss Julie: We made love. I must mean something to you.

Jean: With a child's innocent eyes, I loved you.

Miss Julie: That's when you used to spy on me.

Jean: *Spy* on you?

Miss Julie: Well now you've acted upon your love. Better late than never.

Jean: That's not exactly what happened.

Miss Julie: Jean, this is no time for a lover's quarrel about who did what and when. Let's go out and walk. You'll feel better in the fresh air. I don't know why it's so hard for men to tell someone they love them.

Jean: I don't want to go outside. Your father may call for me.

Miss Julie: No, you're afraid to be seen with me by the others. One minute you're kissing me and the next you're running away. Like a little boy. You're not being very gallant. I was wrong in thinking you were independent.

Jean: There are limits to what I can do or say around here.

Miss Julie: There wasn't last night. I'm not your boss. Things have changed.

Jean: *(Torn.)* It was stupid what we did. I ruined everything.

Miss Julie: Can't you admit that you have feelings for me?

Jean: I do. But I'm not about to vomit them out so you can lap them up like some hungry dog.

Miss Julie: *(Full of fine Southern composure.)* Can you tell me what's wrong, Jean?

Jean: I won't bare my soul to you. So you can take the upper hand. I'm not going to be another Clem Roberts.

Miss Julie: Well, I would hardly worry about approaching his level.

Jean: I know what you were up to with him in the barn. With that whip. Even though he's a lawyer he had enough self-respect left to walk away.

Miss Julie: *(Still finely composed.)* You still spy on me! He didn't go. For your information, *I* broke off the engagement.

Jean: I won't jump when you say jump. Not if I'm your lover.

Miss Julie: Only if you're my employee—

Jean: Just because your father was no good to you it doesn't mean you have to be no good to all men.

Miss Julie *maintains her composure.*

Miss Julie: I didn't know: you're a psychologist! Now I'm certain there would be no financial worries. You can make upwards of a hundred dollars an hour. Why you work in the fields for peanuts surely escapes me.

Jean: I suppose it's to get close enough to lick the hand of who's throwing the peanuts out for me. *(Pause.)* Well, it was partly my fault—last night. But it didn't help that you were so easy.

Miss Julie: I wasn't easy.

Jean: Oh, come on—

Miss Julie: Is this how you like to charm your lady friends? By insulting them?

Jean: Just stating the facts.

Miss Julie: I can see that you've been only pretending to be nice. Jean, I may never completely understand the Cajun mind.

Jean: Miss Julie. I'm sorry. That was not very nice. Would you care for a drink? Do you mind if I have one? *(Truly frustrated.)* Oh, Jesus. *(He goes to a drawer, opens it, takes out the bottle of wine. He fills a glass for himself.)*

Miss Julie: Where does that wine come from anyway?

Jean: It's from the wine closet. *(He takes a drink from the glass.)*

Miss Julie: Has my father given you permission to drink it?

Jean: Not explicitly.

Miss Julie: Don't you think it would be a good idea to ask him before you take it?

Jean: I don't think he'd mind.

Miss Julie: These things cost the farm money. We're not mining gold here.

Jean: I'm not a lush.

Miss Julie: *(Exploding.)* Are you calling my family lushes?

Jean: No. *(With gentleness.)* Settle down.

Miss Julie: *(Miserably.)* Oh, Jean.

Jean: Miss Julie, you're a fine young woman. To call what we had *love*—it's not too wise.

A long pause. She doesn't know what to do. Jean *carefully sets his wine glass down.*

Miss Julie: You're sure of yourself. I envy that.

Jean: *(Pause. Gazing at her.)* Oh, Julie, you're so beautiful. Once you've set a man on fire, there's nothing he won't do for you. *(He swiftly grabs hold of her and takes her into his arms. He kisses her almost violently.)*

Miss Julie: I can't. Let me go.

Jean: Why?

Miss Julie: Jean, because you're hurting me. *(She breaks away from her. They face each other, looking tensely into each others' eyes. The* Last Dancer *enters.)*

Last Dancer:
> A land without strife
> Is a land without life.
> How so much is caused by desire,
> By fears not always clear,
> Don't be foolish and try to make them disappear,

> They are here, you're here,
> There's no stealing away,
> Resolve to find a better way...

The Last Dancer *stands aside.*

Miss Julie: *(Evenly, almost mechanically, to Jean.)* I'm afraid, but I'm not afraid of you.

Jean: *(Pause. Evenly, like* Miss Julie.) I have no reason to trust you. I mean, in any deep sense. All you want to do is toy with any man that comes into your life.

Miss Julie: *(Again, evenly.)* That's how you get your thrills. By putting your thing in, bringing the high down low. It's not sex, it's getting even.

Jean: Can't there be a middle ground?

Last Dancer:
> The land with life is here, you're here.
> I must go.

The Last Dancer *exits.*

Miss Julie: *(Agonized.)* Tell me what to do, Jean.

Christine *enters. She is dressed for church.*

Christine: Someone phoned. Miss Julie, your father's not coming back today. It seems he had too much to drink last night.

Jean: *(Glancing towards* Miss Julie): He's not the only one.

Miss Julie: *(Wounded by the remark.)* Help me, Christine—help me against this man! You're a woman and you're my friend. He has no shame, no discretion.

Christine: I know what you've done with him. You get what you deserve.

Miss Julie: You know he's a monster—

Christine: You're both in the same league as far as I'm concerned. I'm going to church. And soon you'll have to find someone else to look after the house.

Miss Julie: Don't leave me, Christine. I never meant you any harm. *(Brightening up, but still desperate.)* Why don't the three of us sit down and talk?

Christine: Oh, it's beyond that.

Miss Julie: *(In agony.)* Everything's starting to turn gray...

Jean: *(To* Miss Julie.) Don't think you'll get us to pity you.

Miss Julie: No— I'm not well. I'm really not.

Christine: Goodbye. *(She starts to leave, but then turns around.)*

Vipers. No, vampires,
Living in darkness, cut off from life
By the sharpest, blackest knife.
You're with the selfish, the dead.
You'll take no more blood from me. *(She exits.)*

Jean: Notice she didn't say anything about how she skims off a little money from the groceries now and then.

Now the vipers can rest in their nest. Do they mention vampires in the Bible? I don't consider myself a vampire, do you? (Miss Julie *does not respond.)* I'm going to get some garlic—a few cloves to chew, the rest to hang around my neck. That'll keep you away from me.

Miss Julie: Why are you turning on me?

Jean: You could've tried to stick up for me. She was my fiancée. You know?

Miss Julie: *(Pause.)* I will have a drink after all.

Jean: *(Almost taunting.)* There you are.

Miss Julie: Please.

Jean: *(He pours wine into her glass. He watches her take a drink.)* It'll soothe the pain.

Miss Julie: What's going to happen to us? *(Jean shrugs.)* I'll make my father send you away. I can't pretend to live here in peace when you refuse me.

Jean: You do misunderstand me when you talk about *love.*

A sound off stage is heard.

Miss Julie: I don't give up. *(Another loud sound of someone in the next room is heard.)* What's that?

Dad, *a huge, thin spectacle of a man, is played by the dancer who played* Mia. *The actor is in a life-size puppet outfit—or otherwise unnaturally dressed, perhaps wearing a mask, wearing elevated shoes, and the like.* Dad *walks in, wobbling, drunk, yet imposing.*

Miss Julie: Hello, Dad. I thought you weren't coming back today. Who gave you a ride?

Dad: Ride, ride? *(Pause.)* All the influences working beneath the sky: think of *broad action,* the *common nature* of these influences combined—even in spite of the tendencies of each smaller affect.

Just as a quick spark of lightening in the distant mountains may activate forces that decide the issue of life or death downstream—an unforeseen incident on the coast may trigger an otherwise impossible appearance by Yours Truly on his farm.

Miss Julie: Well, you're back.

Dad: Terry Kirkland had to come this way. He ran out of propane.

Jean: Would you like to sit down, sir?

Dad: It's the warmest the earth has been for one hundred thousand years. Make the best of it, I say. We had a fire of driftwood last night. I wanted my bed by the ocean, on the sand. While we still can. 'Would've liked to cuddle up with the radio. They don't play opera but only in the afternoon. I could weep a thousand tears for any woman that Verdi ever created. Weep tears as big as apples. Wagner's not for the heart, only for the mind. *(To his daughter.)* You used to like *(He draws out this word.)* Götterdämmerung, didn't you? *(Pause.)* Used to be nothing could stay open on Sunday—Jean, you know. *(He looks at the wine bottle.)* I see; be sure to take the whole day off. We've got a full week of work ahead of us. I'm going to bed. *(He wobbles off, exiting the stage.)*

Jean: He can tell.

Miss Julie: You're afraid of him.

Jean: A little fear can help you survive.

Miss Julie: I didn't have anything to live for before last night. I would've killed myself if I'd hadn't been with you.

Jean: *(Facetiously.)*I didn't know how much your father lifts your spirits. *(Pause.)* I see how you want to fly up and away. With eagle eyes, you want to look down from above. Yeah, and swoop down and maybe tear something apart from time to time.

Miss Julie: I feel very sick now. Excuse me.

She goes out. Music, not blatantly ominous, yet serious all the same, is heard. It gets louder. Jean looks out the window. He then walks over to the counter and leans against it. The Four Dancers *enter. Their movements are simple as they make their way to the place on the stage where they will build their "falling sculpture". The music plays and Jean watches. The* Four Dancers *take turns mounting each other to represent a falling action; there are some attempts to "fly" as well.*

At the end of this dance, the music fades out and the Dancers *leave.* Jean *is left alone on stage. Pause. He looks out the window)*

Jean: With eagle eyes, she wants to look down from above. *(He paces a little, he thinks.)* It is a pity.

The Chorus *enters; one half of it speaks and is answered by the second half.*

First Half of the Chorus:
    She climbs out of the barn's top window

Second Half of the Chorus:
    There's a magnolia below,
    And a small princess tree, too.

First Half of the Chorus:
    She climbs up on the roof
    And picks her way across the shingles,

Second Half of the Chorus:
    Yellow roses to the side below,
    By the big red barn.

First Half of the Chorus:
    She crawls around to the top
    And reaches the highest point:

Second Half of the Chorus:
> She throws herself down
> Into the yard below.
> We reckon it was fifty feet in all.

First Half of the Chorus: She got caught by the tree.

Jean: Did she survive?

Whole Chorus: We will see.

The Chorus *exits.* Jean *resists going outside to investigate. Intense music. He looks up at the ceiling of the kitchen in anguish. Pause. The music fades. The* Chorus *enters carrying the motionless* Miss Julie *on a stretcher. They place the stretcher on the ground.)*

Whole Chorus:
> The shade tree, the tree of life, it was.
> It broke her fall.
> Yes, she survived.

Miss Julie *gets up out of the stretcher and brushes herself off. She speaks to the audience:*

Miss Julie: I'm out there in the yard still, lying on my back. You don't move a person from where they are, after they've fallen. You wait for proper medical attention. They've called an ambulance—it's on its way. My father has been told. It hasn't made a dent in his mind: he's flat on his back, like I am, only he's drunk, passed out, in his own bed.

I know I shouldn't have tried to fly. But I did what I did, it's best not to move anyone who's fallen from so high. You could further hurt them.

(Pause.) Once upon a time, a Julie would have died. There'll be no undertaker this time. We live in an age now

where more Julies are likely to survive. Better mental health facilities, at least in the good old United States.

(To Jean.) What will I do, Jean? What would you do if you were me? Why can't you say you love me?

Dad believes it's all going to be flooded for good—one day. We don't know when. We've just got to wait and see. How much of his beliefs should we factor in?

Is this what they mean by quality of life?

Miss Julie *walks off the stage. Music begins. The lights fade to black and the play ends.*

The Babysitter

and its afterpiece:

Germany

Dislocations. Hallucinations. Through them all the characters in *The Babysitter* engage in a risky, dark buffoonery. Opportunities for cartoonish music and sounds abound. From time to time throughout the play, Debbie and Stettbacher make movements that are in unison; these are important visible bonds for the audience, for rational explanations may fail us when we try to tell why these two are still married to each other.

Stylized acting in the more searing emotional sections is necessary—*The Babysitter* is not a melodrama. Elements of vaudeville and magic-show showmanship should be explored and incorporated into the performance when possible. Character-wise, Stettbacher has some kinship with Hjalmar Ekdal of *The Wild Duck*, Edgar Valpor of *The Water Hen* and Willy Loman of *Death of a Salesman*.

The action of *The Babysitter* moves to flush out the toxins inferred in the play. The cathartic action of *The Babysitter* fails; no one gets clean, characters are only left in limbo and so are we; this condition is what makes *Germany* necessary. *Germany,* with its simple revenge action—note well that all the avengers are played by women—adds definition, a purging action and makes for a wholeness lacking in the presentation of *The Babysitter* by itself.

The Babysitter premiered October 19, 1995 at the Robert Gill Theatre in Toronto. Movement and physical concerns contrary to Naturalism where explored in the performances—for example: Debbie at times moved around the stage like a gunslinger; the Mother had a few inexplicably odd walks in her physical repertoire that she drew upon. The make-up for all the characters except for the Babysitter was indebted to Chinese Opera and Kabuki theatre make-up techniques. Thanks go to Philip Shepherd who served as directing consultant. The play is dedicated to Paul Scallan.

The Characters

Stettbacher	Male, 38 years old.
Debbie	Female, around the same age.
Babysitter	Female, 16 or 17 years old.
Mother	Female, over 35.

Place: A Colorado Springs-area apartment.

Time: 1995.

The Babysitter

The Scene

Inside the living room of a condominium. The literal condo layout is assumed to be something like this: the living room adjoins the bedroom which itself leads to a bathroom. The living room would also give way to a kitchen; the front door of the condo opens into the living room. However all is rendered loosely, without any concern for true Naturalistic representation. Instead, the emphasis is upon inventing a toxic environment.

The lights come up and sunshine streams into the room through a "window". A fragment of a mangled barbecue has come up through the floor of the condo, stage right. Some furnishings in the room are covered with throws. A broom, one object of a military nature, and something like a television, are seen. A large, old rocking chair, incongruous with the rest of the furnishings, is down stage left. It will later be used when the Babysitter slips into the role of Stettbacher's mother. Daryl Stettbacher sits on a sofa, cleaning off a small box of business cards. Debbie stands with a T.V. guide in her hand.

Stettbacher: Three days since the neighbors' brand-new Zeus-neutron barbecue blew up. You can't sweep out grit and sausage residue by opening a window.

Debbie: You mind? I'm reading the T.V. guide. *(She only momentarily lifts the T.V. guide for a glance at it.)*

Stettbacher: I'm shutting it. A cold, that's what you're going to give me.

Debbie: You don't catch a cold by a draft. Germs give you a cold. Like freckles give you the mumps.

Stettbacher: I'm talking about the stress of being in cold air.

Debbie: I like the breeze. Don't tell me about stress. You give it to yourself.

Stettbacher: *(Starting to the window.)* You seem to get it when they talk about holding the line on military benefits.

Debbie: Well, we shouldn't be stopped from getting what we deserve. Don't touch that window. *(He retreats from the window.)*

Stettbacher: Don't get upset.

Debbie: I'm not. You're the one that gets upset. When you lose your num-nums in Europe, and...

Stettbacher: I didn't lose my num-nums, Debbie. *(Pause.)* It's been perfect for you. An early retirement. Home to the States. Oh, and the most important thing—we still get the checks. The checks that you spend in seconds flat.

Debbie *goes over to the box of business cards and takes one out.*

Debbie: This side-business idea really kills me.

Stettbacher: I would like to do something with my time.

Debbie: Captain, you don't have enough strength. Not to frumkin glaizen fuller. Don't bother to advertise—

Stettbacher: Your vote of confidence. ...Look, any God-fearing American truck, car, or van and some aircraft too, can be frumkin glaizen fullered. I'm just filling a need that...

Debbie: Needs, beads. You wake up at eleven. By then I've done more that you do in a week.

Stettbacher: Okay. Undermine me like a knife-wielding submarine— *(Silence.)* You pick on me. Like right now. You take a special joy in thrusting at me with your sharpened periscope. No matter how small it is.

Debbie: *(Muttering.)* Your business'll turn out just like your attempts to learn German.

Stettbacher: Don't mutter to me. *(Mutters.)* Condescending... *(Thinks to himself out loud.)* "Mutter." *"Moo-ter."*—That means "Mother" in German.

Debbie *(Taunting.)* Impressive.

Stettbacher: Well, yes, you know everything. You know how to talk officer's wives' talk. How to walk their walk.

Debbie: *(A huge pronouncement.)* Daryl, I am sick of your non-methyldopa-induced leaning tower of pizza.

Stettbacher: I've been your meal ticket through the Orient, Europe, points south, east and west. Away from your insect-creep of a father.

Debbie: *(Sassy, like angry child.)* You're a lousy set of underpants yourself. *(The doorbell rings.)* Send 'em away. Whoever they are. I'm not home.

Stettbacher: I'm not going to get it. (Debbie *does not budge. Finally he gets up and answers the door. Miffed, under his breath he says:)* Go fly a broom! *(He opens the door. The* Babysitter *enters with a letter in her hand.)*

Babysitter: Hi, I've come to babysit. Ah... Mr. *Stettbacher?* *(To* Debbie.) I spoke to you yesterday on the phone.

Debbie: No you didn't.

Babysitter: *(Glancing quickly at the room. To herself.)* Man, this place is a mess... *(She takes a scrap of paper out of her pocket and looks at it.)* Ten-ten Security Lane, Security, Colorado? This is the right address, isn't it?

Stettbacher: But we live in Unit B.

Babysitter: That's what it says here, "One-oh one-oh Security, Unit B." Oh, I forgot. Here's a letter I found outside. *(She looks over the envelope again.)* Yep, it's for you. It must've fallen out of the mail box.

Stettbacher: *(Distracted by her looks.)* Put it on the table, no, er... put it anywhere.

The Babysitter *tries to hand the letter to him but he ignores it. It falls to the floor.*

Debbie: I never spoke to you. *(The* Babysitter *glances around the room.)*

Babysitter: I hope you don't think I do cleaning 'cause I don't. I smell barbecue. I hope it's not one of those Zeus-neutron ones. *(She walks a around the room, peeks into the doorway.)* So where's the kid, I mean your child? You said it was how old?

Stettbacher: I don't know why you came here at all—there must be some kind of mistake.

Babysitter: In the back room, sleeping, huh?

Debbie: No.

Babysitter: You guys are military people, right? Some of my best customers are. ... I don't know if I'll ever have kids. *(Pause.)* You people are lucky. You can afford kids with your government pay and all, and you get respect.

Debbie: You should've seen it in the old days. Now that was respect.

Babysitter: Are you in the service, too?

Debbie: My father was. *(Pause. The* Babysitter *looks around the room.)*

Babysitter: Going out this afternoon? A little breezy for a picnic.

Debbie: *(To* Stettbacher.*)* Who is this girl?

Stettbacher: I don't know. Maybe she could do your dirty dishes.

Debbie: She doesn't do cleaning. Can't you hear?

Babysitter: Is anything wrong?

Stettbacher: We're not going out. We're staying right here.

Babysitter: Then I don't know why you need a Babysitter.

Stettbacher: *(To* Debbie.*)* This wasn't my mistake.

Debbie: The weirdest things happen only around you.

Babysitter: The military. My brother's thinking of joining. He wants to fly an AJ-7K. He says it's a lot of carbon fiber.

Stettbacher: I don't know who you spoke to yesterday but we don't need a Babysitter.

Babysitter: If you're not going out, I can understand.

Stettbacher: But you see, there is no baby.

Babysitter: Oh, so his grandma's decided to take him this afternoon.

Debbie: Honey, there ain't no kid.

Stettbacher: We can't have kids now, but in the future— *(In a show of marital happiness, he and* Debbie *move affectionately toward each another, inadvertently trapping the* Babysitter *between themselves.)* ...hmm, Debbie wants a battalion of them.

Debbie: *(Falsely smiling, angry at him.)* "Secrets," squeedums.

Babysitter: *(Breaking away from the couple.)* You really don't have a baby? I could swear when I talked to you yesterday you said...

Stettbacher: It's just Debbie and me.

Babysitter: What about the address? This piece of paper here? *(She fishes out a piece of paper out of her pocket.)*

Stettbacher: I don't know.

Babysitter: My mother screwed this up.

Debbie: *(To her husband.)* Did you have some kind of vaseline on your brain when you contacted this girl? Denny Dallas told me at the base that he cares about your health but it makes him uncomfortable to be around you. Especially when you're thinking.

Stettbacher: So you've been seeing Denny?

Debbie: *(Staring straight at the* Babysitter.) Daryl, apologize for having this girl come all the way over here. Then turn on the stock car races and veg out.

Stettbacher: *(Forced pleasantness.)* The two-hundred's going to be on, little carrot. I want to watch the five-hundred. *(To the* Babysitter.) I apologize for any bridges over bodies of water.

Babysitter: *(Pause.)* My brother's like that. Landlocked in New Mexico. He was doing peyote buttons and realized that people of our generation should also fly the AJ-7K. (Stettbacher *gestures like he is a flying jet or plane.)*

Stettbacher: Great.

Debbie: Honey, they're not going to let him enlist if he's been taking drugs.

Babysitter: They don't give you lie detector tests, do they?

Debbie: Call your Mother and tell her there's been a mistake. *(Pause.)* No. I'll take you home. I need to get out of here. Before we start our spring cleaning. Let me get myself ready to go.

Babysitter: Thanks. *(Pause.)* I don't want to deal with my mother now. I'm afraid I'll *swear* at her.

Debbie: No problem. Have some pop.

Stettbacher: *(Nervously.)* Yeah, I'll get you some pop while you wait. (Debbie *leaves.* Stettbacher *exits within and says, off stage:)* Is Tab okay?

Babysitter: Great. *(He returns carrying two oversized plastic drink containers—perhaps one foot high each—with large protruding straws; The containers and straws are of fluorescent colors.)*

Stettbacher: Hope you like lots. All our glasses are dirty. Debbie and I each have one of our own. *(He holds up the containers; "Daryl" and "Debbie" are printed in large letters on them.)* You can drink out of Debbie's. *(He hands her one container and takes the other for himself. She sits down on the sofa.)*

Babysitter: Thanks.

Debbie: *(Off stage.)* Daryl, did you take your pills? I haven't seen you take any lately.

Stettbacher: *Embarrassed, yelling back to her.)* Oh, you mean, my aspirin? *(To the* Babysitter.) If you don't finish it, you can take it with you in the car when you go. *(He sits down. Left alone with the* Babysitter, *he stammers, hesitates, from time to time.)* So, uhm. Tell me, what's it like? I mean, it's been so long since I've been a kid. Your age. My sister's got some kids. It's nice what they do. What kinds of things do you do?

Babysitter: *(Sips on drink.)* Just trying to graduate, that's all.

Stettbacher: My fly's unzipped. *(He puts his hand to his fly.)* No it isn't. *(Pause.)* Enjoy being a kid while you can. You might grow up and write several computer manuals. For the Army Corps of Engineers. Then meet a girl. I mean, a man. You might instruct at West Point and get decorated later. For being in a conflict. It doesn't matter. There's always somebody who's going to stab you. Just to get ahead.

Early retirement. That's the answer. *(Muttering.)* those... *(Pause. Now musing.)* I was happy as a kid but I'd look for my parents and I, I couldn't find them.

Babysitter: My folks aren't like that. They try to run my life. "Get a job." "No, no. Be home by six." Then they're always grounding me after they hound me.

Stettbacher: She's always bleeding me, to take the seed from me. *(Barking like a dog.)* Grr... ruff-ruff. *(He smiles, pleased with his imitation.)*

Babysitter: Are you okay?

Stettbacher: Parents, the policemen of your world. At least that's what the police hope. But, child, you've got God watching over you. Grow up, you're treated worse than a dog—that's God spelled backwards. *(Pause.)* You know that. You go to school. You learn to read and write.

Silence. Finally:

Babysitter: Yep. *(Pause.)* I got a "B" in American Lit. last year. I could've gotten a "B plus" if only I had perforated my nose.

Pause.

Stettbacher: Your ears. Like my mother's family. They got the ones that stick to the side. Of the face, I mean.

Babysitter: Oh?

Stettbacher: I can still pull duty.

Babysitter: *(Confused.)* Well, I... *(His body contorts. The* Babysitter *at first pretends not to notice.)*

Stettbacher: *(Disdainfully.)* Car races. *(Hopefully.)* Now that you're back...

Babysitter: Back? *(His body contorts again.)* You don't look so good.

• 83

Stettbacher: Foreign lands. Strange lands. I liked it. *(He wipes saliva out of the corner of his mouth. The lights dim, with emphasis.)*

Debbie: *(Off stage.)* It'll be just a little while, I've got to rinse my hair.

Babysitter: *(Surprised.)* What? Rinse your hair? *(The sound of water running in the shower is heard.* Stettbacher *appears to restrain himself from vomiting.)* Jeez, Mr. Stettbacher are you feeling...? *(To herself.)* I've seen some weird things being a babysitter. *(To him.)* You look like your face is turning colors.

Stettbacher: *(Mimicking his wife.)* "Got to rinse my hair, did you take your pills?" *(Now back to his normal voice.)* They first treated me with an excess of adrenalolitaphosphate. Bad medicine. *(He shudders. then looks desperate.)*

Babysitter: *(Alarmed.)* Really, I tell my brother I've seen a whole lot for a person my age because of all the sitting I do.

Stettbacher: I went to a quack who injected oatmeal extract into my pelvis.

Babysitter: Mr. Stettbacher, let me get your wife to...

The sound of the water running in the shower has faded out. Through gestures and changes in voice, Stettbacher *quickly regresses in years. With the first line he is 24 years old. With the next line, 16 years old. Next he is 10, then 6.*

Stettbacher: I had a sister like you. For a week or two. We liked to eat Quaker Oats. Not the instant kind. *(With these next words young Stettbacher means, "You're not my sister".)* Not sister. *(Something about the* Babysitter *reminds him of his mother. His voice turns gradually into that of three-year-*

old boy.) Can you, can you, can you....*(Now he is a child who sings.)* Can you, can you, can you? *(Ad lib:)* Can you, can you... *(He stops singing.)*

Babysitter: Did you say you taught at West Point? What state is that in?

Stettbacher: *(In a child's voice.)* Can you pull your top up? *(The* Babysitter *lets out a little scream. Debbie, in the bathroom, cannot hear it.)* Milk, milk. *(He smacks his lips.)* Mama. *(The* Babysitter *clears her throat. She is alarmed.)* Pee-pee. Daryl pee-pee. (Stettbacher *grabs his crotch, goes over to a wall, walking sideways on one foot. He wants to urinate, but he stops.)* Ow. I can't. *(The* Babysitter *instinctively starts for the front door to leave. But she trips on a chair with throw-cover over it. She skins her leg; She remains on the floor.)*

Babysitter: Oh, God. Man. *(She feels her leg.)* You people are living in a friggin'... *(Pause. Then shouting:)* Mrs. Stettbacher, are you almost ready!?

Again, Debbie *is out of earshot.* Stettbacher *is preoccupied with his foot for some reason.*

Stettbacher: *(Tries to pronounce "shoe".)* Sue. Sue. *(He grabs his crotch, then approaches the seated* Babysitter.*)* Him feels nothing now. *(He limps over to the window and closes it.)* Mommy, I can't sleep wit big wright on. *(He pulls the curtains. The room darkens. Lights remain on* Stettbacher. *The* Babysitter *stays on the floor in pain. He picks up a broom. He tries to stay off the one foot that bothers him. He turns to audience as he is examining the broom and says:)* Maj-rick, maj-ick? *(Stettbacher is trying to say "magic".)*

Pause. Music starts. The Babysitter *slumps, bows her head. She appears to be in a hypnotic state. A cuckoo clock "strikes" three and one half times.*

Stettbacher *lays the handle of the broom he is holding on the Babysitter's shoulder. He handles the broom like a wand or dubbing sword. As he dubs her, glitter rains down on her, with the appropriate accompanying music. He then extends his hand to her and helps her up onto her feet. He sets down the broom. He goes down on his knees and clasps the Babysitter's knees. In a motherly fashion she pats him on the top of the head. But this does not last long—she turns away from him.* Stettbacher, *using gestures only, pleads for more attention. The* Babysitter *breaks away from him. She goes and sits in the rocking chair.* Stettbacher *gazes at the broom.*

Stettbacher: Womb. Bwomb. *(More light on the* Babysitter, *who is transformed. She sits in the rocking chair and she begins to hold an imaginary baby to her breast. The music continues.)* Mommy, me, me— *(He bends down and pulls off his shoe. He draws a piece of wood out of his shoe. This is what has been irritating him. He holds the wood piece up in the light. The music plays. He marvels at it.)* What this?

Babysitter: *(In a severe mother's tone while she is in character as the mother.)* Put your shoe back on.

Stettbacher: *(Still marveling.)* A widdle piece.

Babysitter: You tracking all sorts of garbage in again? *(Pause.)* Your daddy gave you that shoe. *(He stops holding up the large splinter.)*

Stettbacher: Where daddy?

Babysitter: Your sister's sleeping now.

He is worried. Music continues. He looks at audience members and asks them:

Stettbacher: *(Twice or three times.)* Who are you?

Babysitter: Get me that soda pop, would you? Or I'll hit you. I'm thirsty. Your baby sister's going to need her milk.

Stettbacher *hands her the container. She drinks and gives it back to him. He sets the container down.*

Stettbacher: Dair. I wanna suck like baby sucks.

Babysitter: You're too old.

Stettbacher: When you gonna let me come home?

Babysitter: You can stay out as long as you want.

Stettbacher: I don't want. You're no good mommy, just like Debbie. *(The music starts to fade. The* Babysitter *looks at the imaginary child she is holding. Pause. He looks desperately at the* Babysitter.*)*

Debbie: *(Off stage.)* Okay. Just about ready.

Stettbacher: Don't hate me. I need you, mommy, I need you. *(The music ends. He throws the wood splinter at the* Babysitter. *He bursts out in child-like laughter when he realizes he has angered her.)*

Babysitter: You're trying to put my eye out! You little bastard. Stand in the corner.

Stettbacher: *(Bursts out in tears.)* Don't hate me. I need you. I need you. *(He sobs. She makes no effort to comfort him.)* Need, need, oh....

Debbie *enters, with her hair slicked back.*

Debbie: I should've known you couldn't be trusted out of my sight for more than two minutes! *(She marches over to the window, hauls open the curtains. The lights come up. Stettbacher runs and picks up his shoe. He darts out of the room.)*

Debbie: Has my husband been trying to play one of his sick little games with you?

LANCE TAIT

Babysitter: *(Coming out of a fog.)* I don't know exactly what happened.

Debbie: *(Taunting her husband, though she cannot see him.)* Where are you going, Daryl? *(To the* Babysitter.*)* Reduced to a little boy. At least he hasn't lost his sex altogether. *(Looks off stage.)* He's down into the potty training stage now. Out of control. It's not my fault. No, siree. *(Pause.)* My husband and his "stress". Hah. He takes one look at you and ...wow! *(Pause.)* One day I ought to get some diapers in the house. *(With a nod to the bathroom.)* In case he doesn't make it all the way there. *(Pause. She feels around in her pockets.)* I can't find my keys. No. We'll have to get Daryl's set. *(Yelling.)* Daryl, I need your keys.

Stettbacher: *(In adult voice, off stage.)* Not what I need!

Debbie: *(Yelling.)* What? *(We hear the toilet flush.)*

Debbie: Where do you live anyway?

Babysitter: Over on Zeppelin Street. *(Pause, examining herself.)* Jeez, I almost split open my leg. On that thing. A barbecue.

Debbie: Is it cut?

Stettbacher: *(Off stage.)* Not what I need!

Debbie: *(Bellowing.)* Daryl, get a move on! We don't have all afternoon. *(To the* Babysitter.*)* I'll get you a band-aid.

Babysitter: No, that's okay. Don't bother him in the bathroom.

Debbie: His name is Daryl Ulysses Stettbacher. He got a chance to get back with his people. Germans. Hermann was all he got. Hermann was one of those nuts who would creep all over the place and leave Christian leaflets. In buses. In trams. Around the city of Frankfurt. Daryl went A.W.O.L. for a while. He and Hermann shared french fries and beers on park benches. Hermann was a Nazi in World War 2. You meet history on the hoof when you're away in the service.

Babysitter: Your side of the story's interesting.

Debbie: In Germany, Daryl's performance really went to pot. (*Pause. They wait for* Stettbacher.)

Babysitter: What's taking him so long? (*Pause.*) He isn't well.

Debbie: Yeah, sure. (*She rolls her eyes upward. Pause.*) He thinks I should make him better (*She means, "heal him".*) I've got my things to do. I can't leech off the system funded by low wage earners like yourself. I shouldn't have to do that forever.

Babysitter: (*With deep understanding.*) It must be hard for you both to be unemployed, not to mention, emotionally, pretty way out there, too.

Debbie: (*Spoken with relish.*) Oh, you haven't seen anything yet. I'm going to go in and get the keys.

Stettbacher *enters, nearly tearing off the bedroom door. He has an Army hat on. He brandishes a pistol. His manner with the gun is menacing; the* Babysitter *makes no attempt to escape.*)

Stettbacher: Not what I need! All right, Debbie. Assume the position.

Debbie: (*Scolding him.*) Not here.

Babysitter: Oh, no, a gun!

Stettbacher: *(To* Debbie.) I mean it. On your hands and your knees. *(Pause.)* Live ammunition.

Babysitter: Jesus, it's a gun. A gun. In all my years as a...

Stettbacher: *(To the* Babysitter.) I'm sorry it's had to come to this. *(To* Debbie.) I'm going to teach you a lesson.

Debbie: Daryl, not now. There's a girl here.

Babysitter: *(Wailing.)* A gun.

Stettbacher: Actually, a pistol.

Babysitter: What would my brother do?—Holy Pulp Fiction! *(Batting her eyes seductively, then loudly cooing:)* A gun!

Debbie: Don't worry. He'll only harm me.

Babysitter: Mr. Stettbacher. *(Pause.)* I've got to go. I'll walk home, okay?

Stettbacher: *(To the* Babysitter, *waving the pistol mildly.)* Nope. Stay.

Babysitter: I'm sure your wife didn't mean to say anything to upset you.

Stettbacher: How would you know? *(To* Debbie.) Not what I need! *(To the* Babysitter.) Thanks for reminding me. This time I have the benefit of a witness. *(To* Debbie.) Do as I say. *(To the* Babysitter.) Too bad for you your mom dropped you off here. But good for me. With you here maybe I can get what that stupid therapist would call "closure."

Debbie: This won't make anything stop for you.

Babysitter: It isn't happening. All of this isn't happening. Now a gun...

Stettbacher: *(To* Debbie.) Thanks for being a real supportive wife. I said, down! *(The* Babysitter *momentarily considers trying to flee out the front door.* Debbie *is forced down to the floor by the gun. She lies on her back. To* Debbie.) I can cut you in half. *(He momentarily assumes the role of a magician. He requests from his female assistant, that is, the* Babysitter:) Miss, the saw. *(To* Debbie.) Don't move. Don't even try.

Suddenly Debbie *kicks the gun out of her husband's hand and deftly gains control of the gun—and the situation.* Debbie *points the gun at Stettbacher's head and with the gun's barrel she guides him down to the floor.* Stettbacher *is on his hands and knees. She still trains the gun on his head.*

Debbie: The Babysitter and I have decided you've been a bad boy.

Babysitter: Who, me?

Debbie: The Babysitter...

Babysitter: I never...

Debbie: ...and I have decided you need too much. We've decided you've got to strip.

Babysitter: What? Please, put away the gun. *(Pause.)* I want to go home.

Debbie: *(To the* Babysitter.) Don't we all. *(Pause.)* The Babysitter and I have decided strangling's too good for you. The Babysitter and I have decided, that when I defecate, a padded seat is preferable to a wooden one.

Stettbacher: *(In agony.)* Let the girl go.

Debbie: Okay. Let's wait. A minute. (Debbie *kicks off her shoes.*) Now. Clip my toenails!

Stettbacher: Please—

Debbie: Oh, I forgot to bring out the clippers. You'll have to use your teeth.

Stettbacher: *(Moaning.)* No—

Babysitter: Mrs. Stettbacher, can't you work this out some other way with him?

Debbie: Absolutely not.

Stettbacher: *(Totally subjugated.)* Where do I put the clippings, I mean the pieces?

Debbie: *(Spotting the envelope that fell to the floor earlier.)* Put 'em in that envelope or eat them if you want. *(A short drum roll sounds.)*

Stettbacher: The envelope, please.

The Babysitter *is allowed by* Debbie *to pick up the envelope. The Babysitter hands the envelope to* Stettbacher *with a flourish. The drum roll ends. He opens the envelope. A thank-you note and another little card drops out on the floor.*

Stettbacher: From my niece, Sarah. *(Reads.)* Thank you for the birthday. Uncle Daryl, I love you. Love me? *(Tears well up.)* God bless you. *(He looks at the contents of the envelope with great feeling. However the next words are delivered crisply, without melodrama.)* She's only nine years old. Nine years. *(Pause.)* Look, a little drawing of camels, giraffes.... she's sent me. Ah, a half of a bookmark from her church. It's got the face of an angel on it. *(He is greatly moved, but he continues to deliver his speech without melodrama.)* The simple loving world of a child. Her handwriting: wonder, innocence. She reaches... she reaches out with kindness and need... and need. All she wants is... love.

All you, all you want and all they want is to crush me. What a horrible, horrible world. *(He cries.)*

Debbie: *(Waving the gun.)* Get on with it.

Stettbacher: *(Still looking at the card.)* X's and O's for hugs and kisses. *(He throws down the contents of the envelope.)* No more hormones! No more pain! No more pills! No more pain! *(Chants.)* No more hormones! No more p...

Babysitter: Mrs. Stettbacher, you can't do this. Your husband and you—you're victimizing me worse than the Federal government with its trillion dollar debt. *(She turns to the audience:)* I see many taxpayers out there. Maybe we should get one of them up here and do a trick.

Debbie: No. Other things must be done before you and I pick out the new wallpaper.

Babysitter: What did I ever do to you?

Debbie: To tell you the truth, it's what you haven't begun to do for me yet.

Babysitter: I'm only a Babysitter.

Debbie: But you can be so, so much, much more. *(The doorbell rings.)* You have your whole life ahead of you.

Stettbacher: The simple loving world of a child. What a horrible, horrible world.

The doorbell rings again. The Babysitter *runs for the door and flings it open.* The Mother *walks in, self-absorbed. She has a Welcome-Wagon bounce to her voice.*

Mother: I'm so sorry. You're the people with that old back-to-the-basic frumkin glaizen fuller business, aren't you? I mixed your address up with the one I was supposed to take Christine to for her babysitting job.

Babysitter: Great one, Ma.

Stettbacher: *(Getting up.)* We were just looking for Debbie's contact lens before I go to work. My real job is...

Babysitter: *(Interrupting.)* He's sort of in the army. (Debbie *puts the gun down on the chair.)*

Debbie: *(Smiling.)* The reserves, now.

Stettbacher: We have pistol practice today. *(He picks up the gun in a relaxed way, somehow trying to emphasize the point. Stupidly, he waves the gun around in a carefree manner, scaring the daylights out of the women.)* Debbie was hanging on to my gun while I scan the carpet with my eyes. (Debbie *starts to put on her shoes.)*

Debbie: A bee got into my shoes and stung me. Actually a hornet or a yellow-jacket, I think.

Mother: Looks like you're ready to spruce up your place with some home cleaner. My friend sells Amway, by the way.

Stettbacher: Debbie's a pig, I mean a princess in a poke, and I've tried to put my foot down.

Mother: *(Not hearing.)* I only realized my mistake after the Millers called and asked where their Babysitter was. Then I came right over.

Babysitter: *(Muttering.)* Sure. I almost died a minute ago.

Mother: What's that, dear?

Babysitter: Uhm, Mrs. Stettbacher was going to give me a ride home.

Stettbacher: That's why we were trying to find her contact lens.

Mother: Isn't that nice? Military people are so friendly.

Babysitter: Ma, let's go.

Mother: You've got the other job to go to.

Babysitter: I don't feel like prostituting myself for the middle class anymore this afternoon.

Mother: Oh, phooey. Such ideas. *(To* Stettbacher *and* Debbie.) So I bet you're new to Colorado. We're happy to have you military folks. We've got such a beautiful city, don't we?

Debbie: Yes, you do.

Mother: Denver and Boulder don't hold a candle to the 'Springs.

Stettbacher: We used to live in Germany.

Debbie: That was a real blowtorch.

Mother: Oh, how was that?

Stettbacher: There's no place like Germany.

Mother: Well, we've got Pike's Peak, Cheyenne Mountain, Old Colorado City. Garden of the Gods.

Babysitter: Ma, let's go, huh?

Mother: I think this is the most beautiful place in the world.

Debbie: That's why we put in for... sort of a transfer to here.

Mother: And the minorities are so well behaved.

Stettbacher: I like the jets.

Mother: Not the football team, I hope.

Stettbacher: No. I like them away in the sky.

Mother: Everyone here roots for the Broncos.

Stettbacher: Not football. I mean zoom. Zoom, zoom.

Mother: Isn't that lovely? *(Pause.)* Funny you say that. Christine's got to get over to Jet Wing Drive, pronto. We'll call you tomorrow about having our van frumkin glaizen fullered. *(To* Stettbacher.) Was it your ingenious idea to get back to good old American know-how and sweat? *(Falsely, shallow.)* I hope your business idea doesn't fail.

Stettbacher: *(Pause.)* Tomorrow. We should be around then. Zoom.

Mother: *(All is agreed.)* Super— *(Attempting a joke.)* Bowl. Ha, ha. *(Pause.)* Sorry for the slip up. Hope you find your contact lens. Bye. *(She and her daughter start to leave. To her daughter:)* Aren't you going to say goodbye? You could thank them for the atom bombs.

Babysitter: Do I have to?

Mother: I don't know what gets into you sometimes. *(She opens the door and leaves with the* Babysitter. Stettbacher *and* Debbie *stand eyeing each other. Pause.)*

Debbie: You're still hurt they forced you out because of regulations. On performance. *(He gives her the silent* *treatment. Pause. He goes to the window to watch the* Babysitter *and her* Mother *leaving.)*

Stettbacher: Zoom.

Debbie: The sofa, where we used to bend the back bacon, is only good now for thinking about frumkin glaizen fullering.

Stettbacher: Zoom.

Debbie: You don't talk to me anymore!

Stettbacher: Zoom, zoom, zoom!

Debbie: *(Trying to bait him.)* You bastard. She witnessed it. She may tell.

Stettbacher: Zoom. Germany. I'm moving back to Germany. It's time to go.

Debbie: You missing Hermann?

Stettbacher: Germany. That's where I discovered the wounds. The quiet incisions you'd been making between my legs. For years. Humiliated to the point of no return. But I did return. And this is my story. *(Pause. Lighter, more upbeat.)* I ought to hire a girl like that babysitter for around here. She'll come and go. I'll pay her directly. No marriage contracts. Babysitters—at least half of them are still virgins and know how to do their jobs right. This is the best idea I've had. Even better than frumkin glaizen fullering.

Debbie: *(She gets up and starts to leave.)* I'm going out.

Stettbacher: Pick up a bag of corn chips, will you?

Debbie: I'm going out to flag down the first plane to Las Vegas. I'll get myself a new man out there. Or a new car—

whichever comes first. I look for renewal in the 21st century. But renewal must start on the personal level. This is what I believe.

Stettbacher: Whatever you say, Debbie. Good luck.

Debbie: Luck? Is that all you can say? After a bankrupt life? A marriage?

Stettbacher: Yes, Debbie. I'm a... feminist. *(Pause.)* Zoom. *(Pause.)* Zoom. Zoom.

Debbie: *(While he is zooming.)* I don't like my volunteer job. It's not improving my social life. I don't like your international matchbook collection—it's pathetic. I'm leaving. I won't be back. *(She continues to stand, not leaving. Finally she stamps out. We hear the sound of a jet airplane. Stettbacher's head starts to bother him. It feels as though his head is splitting. He holds his head in agony. The jet sound gets louder and louder. Then all of a sudden it fades.* Stettbacher *darts around the room saying, "Zoom, zoom." Some military music plays.* Stettbacher *leaves off his zooming and marches around the room to the music.*

Stettbacher: March! *(Spoken on the beats.)* Huht, two, three, four. *(Not skipping a beat.)* I said, Ah-huht, two, three, four. *(He marches, leaving the stage briefly. Then he comes back out with a dummy that looks like a cross between himself and a grotesque bug. He nails the dummy with its outstretched arms to the wall. He turns to the other wall of the room and addresses it:)* Goodbye. *(He snaps his fingers. This other wall of the room disappears. He addresses the dummy.)* Ah, that's it. *(Demonstrating to the audience, pointing to the dummy.)* Old me. *(Pointing to himself.)* New me. *(Pause. He glances at where the wall was.)* With her gone, the forces are liberated. *(Points to where he stands.)* New place. *(Gestures to the dummy and frowns.)* Old place. Time for a song. *(Music starts.)*

(Song: *"You Should Have Seen Her Spell"*)

Stettbacher: *(Sings.)*
Now I can finally get a distant look
At how she treated me and what it took
To get me out of the bind and how hard I tried to find
A little sanity to help the whole thing gel.

I guess she was always danger,
A harpy come from hell,
But I thought heaven—
Man, you should have seen her spell.

The song and its music ends. Stettbacher *avoids the gaze of the dummy during this next 15 second pause—a new passage of music plays.* Stettbacher *turns to the dummy, beats his own chest, exclaiming, defending, explaining:*

Stettbacher: New man, new land. *(Pause. A new idea comes over him.)* Once upon a... *(The new idea appears to torture him.)* Aw-oh. *(Pause. Resolutely.)* Story Time! *(He turns momentarily to the audience:)* Now children. Be nice. Old stories where bad things happen. *(Shakes his finger at the audience:)* No, no, no. When I imagine that Debbie is dead... You're not supposed to wish anybody that, no matter how much they ask for it. Least of all your wife. *(Pause.)* When I imagine her dead. Something happens. The miracle of the handkerchief turning into a dove? I wish. Nope, instead, I meet a big hairy monster in a bush. A female with udders, crouching, a large nasty pussy-cat with daggery flames in her eyes. Yes this munster is going to get me. For killing Debbie. I didn't do it really. It's all make-believe but what happens? The munster revenges Debbie. By... biting off my leg! *(Pause.)* Like this. *(He goes to the dummy and tears off one of its legs.)* Ow. Now. you know what it's like to have a bad feeling about doing something you're not supposed to do, even if it's the *old* you. You go somewhere else to forget about it. You want to... vanish! But you can't, the munster comes back and because you didn't square everything away, I mean mentally, the monster chews off your other little leg. *(He goes to the dummy and tears off the other leg.)* Thank God it's only a nightmare. You've been eaten by the big wolf and the wolf is you. *(Pause.)* Children, I am rambling. But be sure of one thing: Save yourself from candy. The end. *(He goes over to the dummy and speaks for the dummy.)* "Soldier, how about cheese—that's tasty too." *(He goes back to where he was standing and talks back.)* What? Another story? In my condition? *(Patriotic music plays.)*

In my mind I see that American Cheese is not really cheese. It's not like the cheese that has pleased for centuries. I know that from being in Germany. Hmm. One more thing. I sat down outside to get my head together. *(Almost no pauses in the delivery of these lines.)* On the steps of what turned out to be the library for the base. A couple of teenage girls. They were at the stage where they *really cared* about every person in the whole wide world. If there was anything they could do to make me happy—short of sex—they'd do it. They caught a whiff of my disorientation. They asked me if anything was *wrong*. I figured they're going vote democrat—for the first few years, anyway.

I did look pretty bad. Thanks, I said but you can't do anything. Then I got up and went wandering. Like an unchained dog. Taking direction from smells in the air. *(He sniffs.)* I stomped on. I tried to remember movies, where people did things, things you couldn't find in your job or get out of your wife. Finally, not enough time. I begged for spare change just so I could establish that the whole world was truly against me I uh.... Huht!, *(He swings to face the audience. He points his finger at different members of the audience to each beat.)* two, three, four. The *whole* world was against me. Not one, or two, but the whole enchilada!

(Pause.) It's then that I came up with frum... frump... kin...
The End *End*. *(The patriotic music ends.* Debbie *enters, from limbo.)*

Debbie: *(To the audience:)* And he's encouraged in his stories by people like you.

Stettbacher: *(Angry.)* At first she claimed to be from a normal family!

Debbie: It was my way of playing hard to get.

Pause. This is limbo. The rhythm of the speeches is not always normal.

Stettbacher: Cars. Light trucks. Vans. Frumkin...

Debbie: ...Glaizen Fuller. With no chemicals. Your hopes and...

Stettbacher: ...Fears, yes I have them. You don't have to make them worse.

Debbie: I know you.

Stettbacher: I've got your number, too.

Debbie: *(Turning to the audience:)* Everyone of you. All you women. Watch it. Don't think you have to please the ones who plunge the grunge. It's a man's world but you'll never win that way. Believe me. *(Pause.)* I come from a family of liars. My father stood me up in the doorway. He marked off the inches I grew. Until I was ten. When company came he distorted the facts of my size for reasons only he can know. I got breasts, he started leering at me. This is my childhood. *(Pause.)* Did you know you can use your imagination to do beautiful things? And I don't mean lettuce and pork arranging. *(Pause.)* I wanted to be smart. And not lie. "When you tell the truth, you never have to remember what it was you *really* said."

Stettbacher: Your second fourth grade teacher, Mrs. Sinclair.

Debbie: I thought when I met my future husband, boy, he's smart. We walked by a stream. He knew the story about baby Jesus being put on a celery stick and floated in the water to hide him away from King Pilate's army. And I was really impressed that my future husband had gone to not only regular school, but Sunday school too, because that meant that maybe he had a heart that had been exposed to something other than measuring up your outsides. And that maybe he had moral fiber. Jesus wouldn't have lasted as long as he did during the salad days without the roles of women in his life.

Stettbacher: Blah, blah, blah. Your weight problem, Debbie. It's showing. Zoom.

Debbie: I've been through so much.

Enter the Mother, *from limbo. Her face is very pale.*

Mother: Ah, the crisp alpine air.

Debbie: *(Surprised.)* What's this?

Stettbacher: You're being robbed. Of equal time to blab on and on.

Mother: One's marriage and sexual practices are strictly private business—to be taken up only in the bedroom or on national T.V. Is this national T.V?

Stettbacher: No. It's hold your nose because it's a stink-a-thon.

Mother: Have you ever tried positive thinking? You seem to be a man so much in need of a...

Stettbacher: Yes, I harbor many, *many* resentments. Yet I'm trying to restart my life. Like a boll weevil, I'm looking for a home, home, home.

Mother: That's a child's song.

Stettbacher: No, a slave song. But most of our old slave songs are sung in the schools by children. Makes you think. Yes, and what about school? And the school teacher who took off all of her clothes in class to demonstrate that we should be proud of our bodies?

Debbie: What about the time you courted me.?

Stettbacher: Boy, she couldn't wait to get the old greasy pole.

Mother: Did you take her around the world?

Stettbacher: For answer to that question you must suffer. In complete darkness.

Stettbacher *holds up his fingers. He snaps them. All lights go out. Pause for a few seconds. Lights come up. Primitive sounding music starts. The* Babysitter *magically appears on the spot. She is costumed ornately. Her skirt reminds one of clothing worn by southwestern Indians. She also wears a cut-off cotton teeshirt which is painted with naked breasts—colorful breasts meant to show that* Stettbacher *has glossy, men's-magazine breasts on his mind. The* Babysitter *looks into the distance and says:*

Babysitter:
　　Out of the darkness came light.
　　Out of the light came green.
　　Out of the green came growing.

The goddess Leahocqocxil strides through the
    mountain-glade ferns
Upon a plateau, shaded by stone, bordered by two
    brooks.
The east brook is sweet, the west is salty.
Her trick is to make humans imagine through them
    both.

(To All:) May I pass on this road?

Stettbacher *is sexually aroused by the sight of the Babysitter.*

Stettbacher: All of my dreams have been nightmares until now!

Debbie: Road. What road? Oh, road. I get it. Flagging down planes. Looking for renewal.

Stettbacher: Zoom. Zoom.

Babysitter: May I pass?

Mother: Don't you recognize me?

Babysitter: Biddy-dee, biddy-bum, biddy-boom.

Stettbacher: Zoom.

Babysitter: Biddy-dee, biddy-bum, biddy-boom.

Stettbacher: *(Rhythmically playing off the words.)* Zoom, zoom.

Babysitter: Biddy-dee, biddy-bum, biddy-boom.

Stettbacher: *(Rhythmically.)* Zoom, zoom.

Babysitter: Biddy-dee, biddy-bum, biddy-boom.

Stettbacher: *(Rhythmically.)* Zoom.

Babysitter: Biddy-dee, biddy—

Debbie *cuts off the* Babysitter *and the little jazz session with* Stettbacher *by firmly placing her hand on the Babysitter's shoulder. Pause.*

Mother: I'm your Mother.

Babysitter: I'm standing on Mother.

Mother: No, darling. How could you be? I'm in a vertical position.

Babysitter: Biddy-dee, biddy-bum, biddy-boom. *(Pause.)* Biddy-dee, biddy-bum, biddy-boom. *(Pause. Faster and faster.)* Biddy-dee, biddy-bum, biddy-boom. Biddy-dee, biddy-bum, biddy-boom. *(Etc. Stettbacher cannot stop from staring at the Babysitter's body. The Babysitter stops after almost running out of breath.)*

It's being repeated over and over again. To move you beyond. So many things repeat over and over again. The beyond. Keys, words, to the great Open. So much I've learned in New Mexico. *(Pause.)* Roger, he's a pueblo. Biddy-dee, biddy-bum, biddy-boom. He gave me the repeating key. It's okay to do peyote. It eases the mind's hinge.

(Pause.) Harmonize. Deep breath. Breathe in. And out. Biddy-dee, biddy-bum, biddy-boom. You can only start to change the world by rising above it first. Dignity is engendered in the whole human tribe when all is joined together in oneness. Give me your hands. *(No one gives her their hand.)*

Mother: Christine, put your shirt on.

Babysitter: Now may I pass?

Stettbacher: Yes. Yes! I mean, no! No!

Babysitter: Roger's cool. He studies German on the side. Hegel the philosopher. My brother introduced us.

Debbie: Daryl and I have decided it's time to leave.

Stettbacher: Tell me about the Indian who speaks German.

Debbie: Daryl and I have decided to go home and eat T.V. dinners and play Chinese leap frog.

Babysitter: Don't be uptight.

Mother: God grant me the serenity to endure what I can change and what I cannot change, please let me have the wisdom to know the difference.

Babysitter: *(To her* Mother.) I'm picturing you as a celestial yam. *(To Everyone.)* Clear all your other thoughts out of your mind.

Mother: Impossible. You're naked. My little daughter's been sleeping with a German Indian. Have you no shame in front of a man of the opposite sex?

Babysitter: Biddy-dee, biddy-bum, biddy-boom. *(Pause.)* This'll get you into it. A poem by e.e. cummings. It's really mine. It's in his style. With some of Roger's teachings mixed in:

> All in a whisper biddy-dee, biddy-bum,
> Goes the harmonizing, biddy-dee, biddy-bum,
> Into the summer golden air.
>
> Softer than sleeping eyes,
> Easy, easy, bee-deasy, bee-deasy,
> Boom, boom, deep into the pale
>
> air
>
> true...

Biddy-dee
>boom.

Biddy-dee
>boom.

Side by side, all in one,
Wish in spirit, gum, gum.

...Three oranges and a bag lunch,
Hey, what a morning, Joe.

Stettbacher: You have a gift.

During the poem, Debbie *has moved off into her own direction. She looks into the distance.*

Debbie: *(Barely audible.)* Thereof she telleth.

Babysitter: *(Referring to the poem.)* What that means is... No, I'm not going explain. You've got to *feel* it.

Mother: Oh, I've never felt before? I evacuated you from my insides and that was feeling plenty.

Babysitter: Biddy-dee, biddy-bum, biddy-boom. *(Pause.)* Biddy-dee, biddy-bum, biddy-boom. Forget about the pain. All the pain.

Debbie: *(In her own space, now audible.)*
Now of the Holy Woman,
Thereof she telleth.

Babysitter: You don't need to go slumming in your past.

Stettbacher: That's a good point.

Babysitter: Please join me. It will cost you nothing—I can't charge you—it's a religious thing. Sure could use the dough. Don't you know. You and your generation are lining up to grab the taxpayer's money even as we speak. Biddy-dee, biddy-bum, biddy-boom. *(Pause.)* Biddy-dee, biddy-bum, biddy-boom.

Debbie: *(Off in her own space.)*
   A richly 'broidered dress.
   Thereof she telleth.

Babysitter: *(Not waiting for* Debbie *to finish.)* Biddy-dee, biddy... All right. *(She will accelerate her speech gradually, in waves.)* Biddy-dee, biddy-bum, biddy-boom. Biddy-dee, biddy-bum, biddy-boom. Biddy-dee, biddy-bum, biddy-boom. Biddy-dee, biddy-bum, biddy-boom. *(In spiritual ecstasy, she cries out.)* If you let it, it can start happening anytime.

Debbie: *(Moving towards the others.)* Yeah, I think I can—

Stettbacher: You're faking it Debbie, you're real good at that.

Debbie: Something's happening. I'm, like... taking off.

Babysitter: Yes, that's it. Biddy-dee, biddy-bum, biddy-boom. *(Pause.)* Biddy-dee, biddy-bum, biddy-boom.

Debbie: Also there's a sound—like far away magnets of... Oh, it's wonderful.

The Babysitter *nods her head in approval and in pleasure at* Debbie *who is getting in the groove.*

Stettbacher: *(Glancing at* Debbie *and the* Babysitter.*)* Ah, yes, the sisterhood.

Babysitter: Hmm. Biddy-dee, biddy-bum, biddy-boom.

Stettbacher: *(His eyes wander over to the* Babysitter's *breasts.)* I can't concentrate.

Babysitter: *(To* Debbie.) You know, you and your husband not having kids—it's the only thing you've done right.

Debbie: You really think so?

Babysitter: People are destroying creation. There is a need for regeneration. But for Nature. Give the human race a rest.

Mother: *(Curious.)* But if sex isn't for procreation that means I might as well be a lesbian.

Babysitter: Mom, we're like a species of multiplying killer bunnies.

Stettbacher: *(Leering.)* Yeah, killer Playboy bunnies.

Debbie: You think we're doomed?

Babysitter: Some are drawn into this world by peyote. *(She means herself. She then looks at her mother.)* Some are drawn into this world because they are a close relative. *(She looks over to* Debbie.) Some are drawn into this world because they believe in the grandfalloon of sisterhoodedness. *(She looks over to* Stettbacher.) Some are drawn into this world because of sex or a search for the earth-mama-goddess they know as breast milk. Whatever first gets you to the world doesn't matter. It's what happens *after* that matters. You understand?

Stettbacher: I'm trying.

Babysitter: *(Pause.)* Get ready. This is an exorcism.

A pause, then:

Babysitter, Debbie and Mother:
Biddy-dee, biddy-bum, biddy-boom. Biddy-dee, biddy-bum, biddy-boom. Biddy-dee, biddy-bum, biddy-boom. Biddy-dee, biddy-bum, biddy-boom. *(Etc.)*

They continue saying the mantra for a half of a minute, then, above the mantra, Stettbacher *speaks:*

Stettbacher: *(Aside.)* There isn't time for all this biddy boom crap. *(To the audience:)* Zoom, you know. Look, I'll tell you. Out here the mountain terrain, the climate... little bits of sand, there's hailstones, and when the rain comes, it pours. That's why I'm starting it up. It's the best fullering and the fastest frumkin you can get this side of the *(He makes a gestures signifying large breasts.)* Grand Tetons. And the other thing is... *(He lowers his voice slightly.)* I think I've got a way to get Debbie both simultaneously out of my hair and at my beck and call. It does involve pills. So I'd better keep it...

Stettbacher *taps his closed lips with his index finger a couple of times. The others continue the mantra.* Stettbacher *joins in:*

Babysitter, Debbie, Mother and Stettbacher:
Biddy-dee, biddy-bum, biddy-boom, biddy-dee, biddy-bum, biddy-boom. *(Etc.)*

Lights out. The mantra and music continue for a moment. The play ends.

Germany

Partly modeled after a Chinese rural folk play.

To be played directly after *The Babysitter*
with no intermission.

The Characters

Ilse   Played by the same actor who plays
                            Debbie.

Rudi   Played by the same actor who plays
                            Stettbacher.

Katrin   Played by the same actor who plays
                            the Babysitter.

Dieter   Played by the same actor who plays
                            the Mother.

Place: After a travel sequence, a house in Leipzig, in former
East Germany.

Time: 1995.

Germany

The Scene

We are in what was once East Germany before the fall of the Berlin Wall. The same set used for The Babysitter *is used. The sofa and other pieces of furniture have been removed, however.*

The lights come up on Ilse, on stage alone.

Ilse: *(Rhythmically, to music.)*
My name is Ilse.
I'm going from Plauen to Leipzig,
To revenge my sister.
In Leipzig I'll find Rudi
There I will smite him.
Rudi, Rudi, Rudi,
A dirtier soul there never was—
He's still going about his business
Like he always does.
Find Rudi, Rudi.

I don't care what happens to me
As long as he
Never again swallows beer.
Rudi, my ex-brother-in-law,
Soon to take a fall.

Pause. The music changes.

Ilse: *(Continuing rhythmically to the music.)*
    The days my sister and I
    Walked along the brook,
    The days we'd both confide in each other
    Are gone—
    Because my sister
    Is dead.

Pause. Music continues, then:

    The people are easily fooled
    And misery is the result.
    The likes of Rudi succeed—
    Those who can must fight back.

    There is a man called Dieter
    Who'll help me in my mission.
    I go to Dieter's house now,
    From there we'll seek out Rudi,
    Lure him into a trap,
    A great big animal trap.

    Well, here's Dieter's house.
    Knocking at the door,
    I remember it's still early
    And Dieter can't yet be home.

Katrin *comes out onto the stage.*

Katrin: *(To music.)*
    Let me take your coat, dear,
    My husband's not returned.
    We're sorry 'bout your sister,
    Sorry for you and her son.
    Is the son out of hospital?
    Is the son out of hospital?

Ilse: *(Still to music.)*
    He's with the father, now.

The music stops.

Katrin: With Rudi? That's horrible. *(Pause. Her rapping or "chanting" stops. She speaks normally.)* My name is Katrin. *(She and Ilse shake hands.)* Ah, that we meet under such circumstances.

Ilse *quickly glances at the interior of the house.*

Ilse: You've moved here from the West?

Katrin:
> Yes. *(Pause.)* I'm opening the door
> Which has an inlaid panel in it.
> Mahogany and oak placed in solid maple—
> Please come in.

Ilse:
> Thank you. *(Coming into the house.)*
> Oh, what a *schoenes* house.

Katrin: We own a construction company. You know our parents were originally from here, from Leipzig. We decided to bring our company to this city after the fall of the wall. Come in. Please—

Ilse: What beautiful window casings you have.

Katrin: Oh, they've yet to be stained.

Ilse: And what a luxurious ceiling fan.

Katrin: This part of town in summer gets very warm.

Ilse: And that picture of river rapids.

Katrin: Rapids? Oh, that—

Ilse: And in back of the house. You have a garden. *(They take a few steps and go into the imaginary garden.)* Outside here the air is fresh and clear. How wonderful—this place.

Katrin: We put the tulips in last year.

Ilse: Tulips in last year.

Katrin: The peonies are doing well.

Ilse: Nicely, yes. The lilies look fine too.

Katrin: Six months ago we made the little fence.

Ilse: Four months ago you planted rose bushes.

Katrin: Yes, you know about gardening?

Ilse: Three months ago, violets. Two months ago you added begonias.

Katrin: You really know about flowers.

Ilse: One month ago, marigolds. Two weeks ago, petunias.

Katrin:
> I enjoy flowers, like you.
> They're blooming—
> Look, they almost vie with each
> To see which is the prettiest.

Ilse:
> You've made your own world here.
> This lemon grass is a good choice.

To the audience:

> I'm thinking, this is all so beautiful,
> But what about the ugly business ahead?

Katrin:
>Here are the beginnings of a small fish pond.
>We'll put carp in, it'll be like a Chinese pond.

Ilse: *(To the audience:)*
>We're looking down into the water and I'm thinking,
>Does she know what I want to do about Rudi?

Katrin: *(To the audience:)*
>Her face, reflecting in the pool of water,
>Shows great signs of worry.

The women go back to speaking with one each other.

Ilse:
>The red tiles of your roof
>Are well fitted—you spared no expense there.

Katrin:
>The crew from my husband's company
>Saw to it that all was done carefully.
>Dieter can tell you more.
>He's also very proud of the house.
>Let's go back in.

In a few steps, the women are back in the house.

>You should sit down
>It must've been a tiring journey
>Would you like some coffee?

Ilse: Yes, thank you. *(She sits down.)*

Katrin:
>If you keep a watch out that window there
>You might see Dieter arrive.
>I'll be out in the kitchen.

Katrin *goes to get the coffee.*

Ilse: *(Pause.)* As I look out the window I think of how it was that I came *here*. You see, Rudi had once used the services of Dieter's company. Rudi never paid him a penny for what the company did. Dieter went to the courts for help.

The courts impounded Rudi's car. The car was to be sold at an auction. But the car that was taken for the auction was really my sister's car. Dieter was supposed to take the proceeds of the car sale as a settlement. But when he found out that Bettina—my sister—needed the car, he called off the proceedings.

Two months later Dieter was beside himself. He locates *me*. He asks me if there's anything he can do. My sister died in a fire at the battered woman's shelter owned by the City of Leipzig. Rudi's suing the city for her wrongful death.

Pause. Music starts up again.

Ilse: *(Rhythmically, to music.)*
I lift up my eyes and look around.
So much seems at the edge of collapse.
Did I also tell you that Rudi,
Rudi was a rat?
By that I mean we've found out
That he snitched on the citizens of Leipzig
For the former secret police—
The East German Stasi police.

Pause.

What's that out the window I see?
More frightening than a ghost.
It's Rudi, oh, it is Rudi,
And he's coming right this way!

Lights change. Rudi's song music begins. Rudi enters.

Rudi: *(Evil, banal, rapping to the music.)*
Got cyclops, got, and got two cyclops eyes,
Got cyclops, cyclops, tough and maximized.
Cyclops rough, and got two cyclops cyclops
Maximized, eyes—over and out!

    In, bitch, in.
    Got, got,
Got cyclops, cyclops, I'm tough as nails.
Got a hammer, kaw, haw, haw.
Got cyclops eyes, too maximized.

I can rip blood out of a stone.
'Can get you chucked out of your home, bro'.
Whining sister, whining mother,
Don't stop me, father, I'm the Other.
    Got, got
Shiny eyes, eyes of knives
Of nine lives.

Sea of fire upon my desire,
They did her in—ember roof collapse,
They'll pay for her,
Her life,
To the maximum.

Sea of fire upon my desire,
They shafted her—up in flames.
Kiss the fire, take the blame,
Pay for her,
My wife,
To the maximum.

You burned her bad,
I want cash for it—
Put it my stash!

Burned her bad,
Give me money for the girl,
Money for the girl, girl, girl.
Money for the girl.

So I can spit on the flame.
(Every limb of Bettina's was steaming in pain.)

Got cyclops eyes, gen-u-wine, gen-u-wine,
Tears in my eyes!
Burning mother, I'm the Other,
Got, got cyclops—eyes and ears!
Got tears—
That burn and burn.

Now that she's in an urn
It's time for me
To earn
The maximum.
Maximum.

Rudi *exits and the music ends.* Katrin *enters.*

Katrin: Is there something wrong? Something to the maximum?

Ilse: Rudi. I saw Rudi. Please protect me from him.

Katrin: There, there, you've had a fright.

Ilse:
His hair was matted down,
His eyes were pitch black glass.

Katrin:
I'll comfort you.
Here, have your coffee.
And keep your mind off dark matters.
Late spring's a wonderful time—

Some new music begins, it is Dieter's music. He enters.

Dieter: *(To music.)*
    Many things are on my mind—
    But of course, the upper most is Ilse.
    ...That woman's terrible state of mind—
    Sorry, sad Ilse.
    Only rage keeps her living.
    Soon we'll be at the place where things are set right.

    What is a man who cannot leave the human scene
    In better shape than it was before he came on that
        scene?

    Katrin, my loyal wife.
    Thank you for caring for Ilse.
    In this world there's no one I trust
    As much as I do you.

The music continues.

Katrin:
    Oh, my sweetheart,
    We are often a picture of wedded happiness
    And it delights me.
    But sometimes I worry—
    I know we have it so well.

Dieter:
    We are lucky, of the few,
    I know it as well as you do.
    Don't be nervous about our happiness.

(The music ends.) Ilse, I'm glad you're here. Welcome to a part of Leipzig that was ranked the worst neighborhood in 1990. Now our city district has been recognized as the "best improved community" in the Over-10,000 population category. We've come a long way. We have good living conditions now, the services, culture... No matter what business is going on here—pizza parlor, bus line—great service and products are available to our people. Just because things have progressed it doesn't

mean we're going to stop trying to improve. The expectations of our citizens are rising. We can do better, we know.

>Having said that, let's deal with the hardness, Ilse,
>The hardness in your heart.
>Soon you will have an easier time of it.
>See how my method assumes the shape of a gun.

Dieter *takes out a gun.*

Katrin: Oh my God, a gun—

Dieter: Don't worry, Katrin.

Katrin: A gun—

Ilse: Yes, a gun.

Dieter: And you thought west Germans were only health food shop types. *(Pause.)* We are sworn to secrecy.

Ilse: Secrecy.

Katrin: Secrecy.

Dieter:
>Good. *(He hands* Ilse *the gun.)*
>A man grown impudent and evil
>Should not only be loathed, but punished.

>As umpires in this game,
>We shall acquaint the offender with our call:
>He is vile; he shall be stopped
>With a speeding lead projectile.

Ilse:
>Sir, that is what I want.
>But I'm afraid my hands will shake
>And my finger will slip from the trigger.

Dieter:
> You'll do the thing
> It'll come naturally.

Ilse: I'm not sure.

Dieter:
> Oh, but I've heard from an old man
> Who served, as a child, in the army in the last war.
> His fingers were tender and mild
> Yet he was able to break life into death's pieces.

Katrin: Where did you get the gun?

Dieter: It was found in the rubble of a building.

Ilse: How can we get near enough to Rudi to shoot him?

Dieter:
> I'll offer Rudi
> Free salvaged material.
> I will lure him to one of our construction sites.
> While my workmen are slugging their hammers at nails
> Or hacking a piece of lumber in two,
> While my workmen are blasting their radios,
> Radios singing, la, la, la,
> Yeah, yeah, yeah, love, love, love—
> You, Ilse, will take the safety off.
> You'll come from behind a wall.
> You'll look into his eyes for the last time.
> You'll fire the luger. Just like that, one, two, three
> Biddy-bum, biddy-boom, biddy-dee.
> He'll fall, he'll die.
> My work crew will take care of the body.
> Let me show you how it will work.

He motions for Ilse *and* Katrin *to sit and they do. He then says to the audience:*

Dieter: And it does go this way, my friends: first we're at the construction site. A man named Hermann drifts in. He tries to convince us that our salvation at the hands of Christ is more important than our hands being used to build better housing for the people of the former German Democratic Republic. Hermann leaves. You, Ilse, have been waiting at the construction site for about an hour—just about the same time it takes Lens Crafters to fit a customer with a new pair of eyeglasses. Soon Rudi appears. Rudi enters. He crosses the threshold of the front door. He comes into the half-finished living room. (Rudi *crosses the threshold of an imaginary front door. He enters the imaginary room.*) He makes a nasty remark about one of workers who is a *legal* alien. He stops, he lights a cigarette. (*After* Rudi *has scowled in the direction of an imaginary worker, he stops and lights a cigarette.*) He asks where the free materials are.

Rudi: You got some materials for me, huh?

Dieter: Yes, I do.

Rudi: So where are they?

Dieter: I've forgiven all your debts to me since I found out that you lost your wife and your boy was badly injured.

Rudi: I never had debts with you.

Dieter: The judge seemed to think you had debts to me.

Rudi: Judges are crafty liars. And weaklings, too.

Dieter: It's a sad world sometimes. I'm glad I have my wife. I don't know sometimes how I could stand it otherwise.

Rudi: You're a real love bird.

Dieter: A woman of only twenty-nine was lost in a fire near this construction site.

Rudi: Just like my Bettina.

Dieter: You put her in that fire.

Rudi: Excuse me?

Dieter: You drove her to her death. In the springtime of her life, as they say. I think that if my wife died, I would want to be with her... and that I would not wait too long to be united with her.

Rudi: You're a crazy love bird.

Dieter: I hear of women who are beaten, abused. There are others besides you who mark Bettina's passing.

Rudi: They're not getting any of the money. Where's the stuff you have for me?

Dieter: Yes, you want your stuff—

Rudi: I do.

Dieter: You're in a hurry—

Rudi: I got places to go.

Dieter: So, you're not relaxed at the moment?

Rudi: Quit playing with me, fool. (*In disgust, he throws down his cigarette and rubs it out on the floor.*)

Dieter: I do have something for you.

Ilse *stands up with the gun. During this speech she and* Rudi *enact her words.*

Ilse:
> As I come from behind the wall
> I've already taken the safety off.
> I close my fingers across the handle of the gun
> I glance and see Rudi.
> A lightning look of surprise crosses his face.
> He has no time to think, to run.
> I see into his horrible eyes for the last time.
> His scared state arouses no pity in me
> I fire at him, the animal.
> One, two, three,
> Biddy-bum, biddy-boom, biddy-dee.
> He falls, he dies.

Rudi *is on the floor, dead.*

Dieter: Yes, but I feel there is something missing in that. *(Pause. To* Rudi.) Get up. (Rudi *gets up. He and* Ilse *assume the positions they were in before she comes from around the wall to kill him.)* It seems to me that you should add more. (Ilse *and* Rudi *follow* Dieter, *pantomiming what he says:)*

> First, you take the safety off.
> You come from behind the wall.
> Rudi is *totally* surprised, number one, that it's you,
> Number two, that there's a gun.
> He greets you and tells you he is glad to see a member
>   of the family again,
> He tells you that he is lonely.
> He reaches out to your hand to shake it, or hold it, or
>   kiss it—
> You wave the gun at him to keep away.
> I tell Rudi softly that he has caused very much pain in
>   the world.
> Rudi doesn't like that.
> You stare with a hard look at Rudi.
> It's the last time you will see his cyclops eyes.
> He's scared but struggles not to show it.
> You have no pity for him.

I take out a knife
I calmly tell him that I intend to carve his liver out of
   his body.
The workmen nearby play their radios
Singing la, la, yeah, yeah, love, love.
You freeze.
Rudi tries to run but I put the knife to his throat.
You attempt to raise your right arm but it's a heavy
   machine;
You cannot move.

Rudi screams but the radio smothers his call throughout the neighborhood. I tell Rudi that no one has forgotten his connections to the former secret police, that this is for them, too. (Dieter *looks squarely at* Rudi.) With this gun now a snitch can be held accountable for his actions.

The pow-pow-pow of the luger rings out. Ilse *has fired the three shots.* Rudi *falls to the floor, dead.*

Dieter: *(Continuing.)*
   You, Ilse, are shaken.
   You drop the gun to the floor.
   You grab me and start weeping.
   I tell you that your sister's death is avenged.
   I say what we've done is right and good.
   Never again will you smell his matted hair.
   I close his eyes
   With the blade of my knife.
   I decide not to cut out his liver.
   My workmen soon dispose of his body.

Music, like that which opened the piece, starts up. Ilse *weeps no more.*

Ilse:

> The days my sister and I
> Walked along the brook,
> The days we'd both confide in each other
> Are gone.
>
> My sister is dead;
> But I have avenged her.
> Her vile husband has been made
> To disappear from this planet.

Pause.

> People are easily fooled
> And misery is the result.
> When the likes of Rudi succeed—
> Those who can must fight back.

Music continues. The lights fade to black as the play ends.

East Play

*(To Deng Xiaoping
in the Great Beyond)*

Everything seems to be a business these days. I would have liked to give this play a title like *Coca-Cola* but I did not want my publisher to be sued.

For the Chinese materials of this play I must acknowledge Shen Tong, a student participant in the Tiananmen protest and Harry Wu ("My personal name is Harry Wu—it's a name for those who have no name. I'm not a hero, I'm just lucky to survive..."). Both men gave lectures that I attended.

I see *East Play* partly as a teaching play, like one of those *Lehrstücke* that writers in Germany wrote between the world wars. But *East Play* gets a little sillier than the German works.

A public reading of this play directed by Michelle Powell—to whom this play is artistically dedicated—was first presented by students at the ArtsFirst Festival, Harvard University, May 2, 1997.

The Characters

Carol   50s-60s, to be played by an actress,
                         20-35 years old.

Prisoner   20s, male.

Jake   Male.

Woman   Female, of child-bearing age.

Boy   Male or female, played by an actor
                         over 60.

Place: An Eastside Manhattan apartment and at the same
time a prison cell in the Chinese Laogai.

Time: 1997.

East Play

The Scene

A finely furnished room in a New York City brownstone. Also a dingy cage or jail cell off to the side, slightly sunken into the floor. Well-to-do Carol, *wearing a priceless jeweled brooch, sits at a table which is set for lunch for one. She does the crossword in the* New York Times. *The Chinese* Prisoner, *in chains, is behind iron bars. At first the lights on the* Prisoner *are low. By the end of the play the* Prisoner *is bathed in light.*

Carol: Jake, come here, please. (Jake *enters.*) I would appreciate it if I saw no more of your Jake's Cakes labels on the bottom of my plates. *(She holds up a plate to demonstrate.)* You are, after all, my butler, and if there is a label to be affixed to my china such a label should read, "T.R.P."—Terribly Rich Presentations.

Jake: An unintentional blunder on my part, madam.

Carol: My brother would think that something's fishy here at Domicile Productions. This is no small infringement.

Jake: I'm nothing but a snake when I'm running Jake's Cakes.

Carol: You're lucky we're on the Eastside, in Manhattan. That you're not in China where you can be sent by the Party to languish in the Laogai.

Jake: And what would the Laogai be, madam?

Carol: Laogai refers to the prison camps of modern China. Laogai is where millions of Chinese people are incarcerated in various degrees of penal servitude. While the masters of China brag about raising the living standards of the country they are throwing free-thinkers into the Laogai. This is what the prisoners in the Laogai make. *(She holds up a cute toy or stuffed animal.)* You can buy these right around the corner, on Madison Avenue.

Prisoner: Laogai. I was a student. In 1989 I dared to speak my mind. In Beijing. In Tiananmen Square. The square at the Gate of Heavenly Peace.

The doorbell rings.

Carol: Is that our neighborhood gossip again? Our local Cup of Sugar Technologies rep?—as she calls herself. All she wants to go is *take over* the place when she comes 'round.

Jake *exits to answer the door. He then re-enters.*

Jake: Madam, we have company.

Carol: *(She can't believe how stupid he is.)* I know.

Jake: A woman and her young son.

Carol: *(Frowning.)* Have we business with them?

Jake: They appear to be strangers.

Carol: What do they want?

Jake: They are selling.

Carol: Selling low?

Jake: Rather high I should think. There is a picture of a large tower on the cover of their prospectus.

Carol: Show them in anyway.

Jake *exits for a moment and brings in a* Woman *and her son. The* Woman, *before she speaks to* Carol, *looks over at the* Prisoner *and bows her head slightly, as if saying a short prayer in silence.*

Woman: Good afternoon, ma'am. I'm so glad you've left your busy schedule to take a meeting with me.

Carol: How do you know I have a busy schedule?

Woman: Doesn't everybody who is part of Unsaved Enterprises?

Jake: *(Whispering to* Carol.) It's a bit unprofessional for her to bring her child.

Carol: *(To the* Woman.) My butler was just saying. How unprofessional it is. To let your child masquerade as a business associate.

Woman: Last night he was visited by Witch Under The Bed Diversified.

Carol: You think last night was rough for him. Look at that prisoner. Every hour is a nightmare.

Woman: I had to sing him to sleep with a psalm.

The Boy *mispronounces his words at times.*

Boy: Mommy, are we at another Spit In My Face branch office?

Woman: Honey, they're not all branch offices of Spit In My Face. Some are branches of Hosanna, Here's a Thousand Dollars.

Pause.

Carol: Don't get your hopes up. *(Pause.)* The Jehovah Agency—that's really the name of your sponsor, isn't it? I've heard that you all twist people's arms till they holler. That will not do at my Domicile Productions. Such behavior is reserved for the Hammerclavier Society. *(Pause.)*

Rather than selling the God Versus the Devil Home Kit you could be doing something which might one day put your son in a place like ... Princeton Success Assured or Harvard Never Loses.

Woman: I've made a contract with the Jesus Alliance. It started on the day I went under water, supported by the loving arms of the Charisma Exploration Group.

Carol: Well, yawn, yawn. Shares still traded of that ancient corporation. *(Pause. To the* Boy.*)* Sonny, do you like cake? *(The* Boy *nods "yes".)* Jake bakes good cakes. Jake, get them one.

Jake *exits.*

Boy: Good cake?

Carol: Very good.

Woman: Usually we eat bread.

Boy: And we pray. *(Pause. To his mother.)* Cake is not the body of the Loard.

Carol: Jake doesn't use lard. *(Pause. To the* Woman.) The cake will only cost you this boy.

Prisoner: She held a banner in her hands.

Woman: *(To* Carol.) Excuse me?

Carol: If you want the cake, you must turn this boy over to me. *(The* Woman *is confused.)* Let him be with me here at Domicile Productions, a division of Terribly Rich Presentations. Let him remain, for a year and a day.

Woman: Cake for a boy? This contravenes the laws of the Ethical Bakers Association.

Carol: So you know about them?

Woman: Since my husband went on the road with Cottontail Entertainment's *Shabby Slut Go Lucky* I've often turned to Ethical Baking myself. Under the blessings of the Big Cross Holdings Group they've helped guide me through my desert. And my dessert.

Carol: Listen, I give you the cake. You give me the boy. I'll set you up as Director of Boulevard Sales for Jake's Cakes since I control that concern—as well as the Ethical Bakers Association, I might add. Once I have your signature I shall take the boy to Europe. There I will have the son that I've never had. By my side. *(To the* Boy.) You may call me Aunt Carol.

Woman: What will you do with him in Europe?

Carol: I'll clothe him in the best industries. I'll teach him how to squander surpluses there. Even though there's plenty of opportunity for that here. He'll learn languages, especially Chinese. China. It's the largest market in the world. And they haven't been fully amalgamated yet. You know, weightloss is their future.

Prisoner: Help me.

Carol: We shall teach China the benefits of endless partnershipping.

Prisoner: You are betraying me.

Carol: I will make your son a model. An oasis of the consumer, by the consumer and for the consumer. He shall inspire the Chinese youth to infinite commodification.

Prisoner: Please, consider my pain.

Carol: And *He* shall head his own firm called Common Fantasy, or See How An Angel Plucked Me Off The Street.

Prisoner: You help them with their repression.

Woman: *(To* Carol.) An *angel* is a sacred being. I don't like the way you're using the word.

Carol: Oh, words. Kicking somebody's more exciting.

Carol *walks over to behind the iron bars. She kicks and beats the* Prisoner. *He yells.*

Prisoner: You place profits before freedom. Because it's more exciting.

Carol: *(To the* Prisoner.) No, sexier. Wake up and buy my roses. *(To the* Woman.) Now. You take the cake. I get the boy.

Pause.

Woman: Okay, it's a deal.

Carol: *(With disbelief and shock.)* You're giving up your own boy?

Woman: We'll make it limited, but not unincorporated.

Pause.

Carol: You break up a trust just like that? No deal!

Woman: I don't know what's come over me. I... I ...

Carol: Something is coming over me. Watch.

Prisoner: Her name was Jilian. She held the banner high.

Suddenly Carol *drops her pose. She takes off the priceless jeweled brooch she is wearing.*

Carol: *(To the* Woman.) I have just tested your strength. It's wanting. I'm not from Terribly Rich Presentations. I'm from Penniless Productions.

We're interested in the human condition. How it's all become a life of business. Even our language is for sale. *We* deal with gestures. Like these. (Carol *makes a few gestures to illustrate the point that strong gestures excite her more than words ever can. One of her gestures might be an imitation of a prisoner being thrown against a wall.)* The stock of our trade. We invest in the Individual. *(Pause.)* I will never be part of the National Union of Stage and Screen Fakers, unless it's just to make money in a movie. Then it's back to Penniless for me—I like the cold shower of fiscal restraint. It keeps the skin taut. Jake, bring the cake out here. (Jake *enters with a cake.)* Now, smash your production on the floor.

Jake: I just made this. Smashing it would be wasteful.

Carol: Set it down, then. We must go.

Stage lights increase on the Prisoner.

Prisoner: *(With conviction.)* I fled to the south.

Jake *sets the cake down on the table. The house lights come up.* Jake, Carol, *the* Woman *and the* Boy *walk out into the audience, perhaps greet some of the spectators, shake some hands, allow their costumes to be touched even. The* Prisoner *remains alone on the stage.*

Jake: *(Demonstrating his intelligence.)* Hong Kong and Taiwan are south.

Carol: You're right about Hong Kong, Jake. It's south. But the Laogai are everywhere.

All actors except for the Prisoner-*actor are entirely off stage now.*

Jake: And what would the Laogai be, madam?

Carol: You've forgotten already? The Laogai are the prison camps millions of Chinese people are forced to work. Some of the prisoners make cute things like this. (Carol *holds up a cute toy or stuffed animal. Directly to the audience:*) Look at the label. If it says, "Made in China", don't buy it. You would be undermining freedom. Don't support people like the late Deng Xiaoping!

Woman: Deng's rule brought China just about to the end of a century that began with the Qing Dynasty.

When little Deng was but a babe in swaddling clothes, there was an infant emperor living in the palace in the center of the Forbidden City. Three wise men came to visit. One was a Confucian who managed a sports team. One was a foreigner who rented Hong Kong. The other was an evaporating witch doctor, who now condenses in our midst.

Jake: *(In a voice not Jake's)*: Stop meddling in Tibet!

Boy: *(In a voice not the Boy's.)* For ages China has been the Uncle of Tibet. The West is trying to break up a family that works.

Woman: *(In a different voice.)* Home-wrecker.

Jake: Hey, wait a minute. Look at the thirty billion dollar project known as the "Three Gorges Dam" on the Yangzi River in China itself. With this, devastation'll be visited upon an area the size of the ancient country of Atlantis.

Boy: Deng Xiaoping visited a rodeo in Houston. It's history now. Deng wore a ten gallon cowboy hat.

Carol: Boy, what are you talking about?

Boy: I thought we were supposed to talk about Deng Xiaoping.

Prisoner:
The army—we thought they were our friends.
Our statement the night before spoke of open debates.

Carol *and* **Jake:** As many as thirty million people perished between 1959 and 1961. Those who share responsibility for the horror remain in power. They continue to visit horror upon the people. Laogai.

Boy: *(In the voice of young China.)* The country's developing fast. Life's better now. But there's a problem: we have no way to pick our rulers. *(In the voice of Western newspapers.)* Can the new leaders manage the world's fastest growing economy? Does the death of Deng open up new chances for democratization?

Carol: Not as long as there are Laogai for people who dare to have their own opinions.

Boy: *(Incredulously, to the audience:)* You expect China to change now or in five years?

Jake: (*Like a voice in an advertisement.*) Wall Street Journal readers want to know.

Carol: I bet they do.

A drum roll, cymbal crash. Martial music then plays. The Boy *speaks above it:*

Boy: (*In an announcer's voice.*) And for the next generation of Chinese rulers, at 70 years old, it's Jiang Zemin. A power engineer turned party boss! He knows some English, likes to quote from the Gettysburg address. (*Pause.*) Or will the leadership be seized by bad Comrade Li Peng, the butcher of Tiananmen Square?

The martial music ends. Other music takes over.

Prisoner:
　　Tiananmen Square, the stretching pavement
　　Of stone, brick, cinders, asphalt.
　　How naive we students were that spring.
　　Red—we thought we still could be—
　　Red—in some loyal sense of the word.
　　My feelings were not as strong as hers.
　　The girl was Jilian;
　　Never before had she done anything like this herself.
　　She was a straight-A student.
　　She held a banner high.

Boy (*In an announcer's voice.*) Deng Xiaoping on economic matters: "We must be bold and make reforms. We must open to the outside. We must have the courage to experiment."

Prisoner:
　　We didn't expect tanks.
　　The troops came directly upon us.

Deng Xiaoping let Li Peng carry out the military
    operation.
But the blood covers his hands too.
Most killings were at the West Gate.
Jilian was one of the first.

Pause. He holds back his tears, then continues:

We had respect for our rulers,
We thought they had respect for us.
When death seemed ten thousand years away
Jilian stood in front
With her long flag held in two hands.
The soldiers opened fire... the banner slips,
Jilian grabs my arm,
She says, "Don't worry
They're only using ...

Pause, the Prisoner *weeps for a moment, then:*

... plastic bullets."
She fell. Her head lay on my foot.

Pause.

Jilian believed, to the end.

Pause.

They gutted the camp in the square.
We ran from that place,
Leaving the opera of youth.
Stifled under the groaning sky.

Boy: *(In the voice of an adult.)* Comrade Deng Xiaoping
liked to be portrayed as one with a superb mental outlook.
He embraced the plain, the simple, and the solemn when
faced with the awesome facts of existence.

Boy: *(Continuing in the voice of an adult.)* Did you know it was Deng Xiaoping who devised the great slogan heard everywhere now? The slogan is, "To get rich is glorious."

Prisoner:
> Rugged months, scary.
> There are many police in the south and finally they
>   caught me.

Woman: Deng Xiaoping, like Chairman Mao, was the son of a wealthy landlord. The spirits of these money changers must be chased out of the temple air.

The music ends. Carol, Jake, *the* Woman *and the* Boy *turn towards the* Prisoner.

Prisoner:
> Now I appear and speak like this in my dreams.
> We have Coca-Cola but not freedom.
> Maybe you too.

Carol, Jake, *the* Woman *and the* Boy *walk back towards the stage. The lights fade to black and the play ends.*

David Mamet Fan Club

For the Girlfriend, who remains nameless, there is in Mamet's dramatic manner a ludicrous descent into the commonplace—in a word, bathos. For Jerry, though, Mamet is an apostle of the pay dirt, worthy of worship. Jerry strains to experience the world as he thinks D.M. does.

I join other playwrights such as Arthur Kopit *(The Road to Nirvana)* and David Ives *(Speed the Play)* in satirizing David Mamet. My play skewers no particular D.M. project—it grazes over the (now academic) field that is Mamet. I use anger to help animate my dramatic characters as I believe Mamet does his; short exchanges between characters à la Mamet are also here: the dialogue on the printed page is spaced in a way that I hope will aid the actor in realizing a pseudo-Mamet style. By the way, I don't think the liberal use of profanity is any guarantee of "authenticity", of being true-to-life; if obscenities crowd a work they seem to me to limit dramatic range.

The reference to John Ralston Saul in the play is to Ralston's book, *Voltaire's Bastards.* The Northrop Frye reference is found in Frye's, *The Well-Tempered Critic.*

The costumes that the two actors wear should have some clownish touches to them. All profanity can be delivered with exaggeration and relish.

A reading of this play was presented by Walter Teres and Pat Hawk at Hart House, University of Toronto, September 19, 1998.

The Characters

Jerry   Male, 30-50.

Girlfriend   Female, Jerry's age, give or take one
                              to ten years.

Place: An apartment somewhere in the U.S.

Time: The present.

David Mamet Fan Club

The Scene

Drum music plays: snare drums, a bass drum—they play "street beats"—successive drum pieces of 8-bars (one 8-bar piece repeating once or twice before moving on to the next 8-bar piece) that the percussion section of a marching band play before or after the brass and winds have joined in for "musical" numbers.

All the necessary props for the play may be on the stage at the beginning of the play. If any props need to be set during the changes "B", "C" and "D", stagehands may assist the Girlfriend in placing them—however Jerry should never lift a finger.

Lights up: Jerry is unshaven. He stands, leafing through a book.

A

The music of the drums ends. The Girlfriend, positioned on the other side of the stage, does not approach him all at once. She keeps her distance at first; as the dialogue is spoken she progressively moves closer to him. By the time the subject of money comes up, she is next to him.

Girlfriend: Ever since you quit your job as a dentist to surround yourself with card sharks, truck drivers and war veterans, you've turned into some freak.

Jerry: *(Preoccupied.)* What's that you say?

Girlfriend: You can still go back to being a dentist.

Jerry: Since you quit the library I've had to *buy* books.

Girlfriend: You weren't so snippety until you got into David Mamet.

Jerry: His journey is my journey. The Truth is important. You agree.

Girlfriend: Not so much any more.

Jerry *puts down the book he's been reading.*

Jerry: Oh. *That's* bothering you. You've been doing some *math* lately.

Girlfriend: We can't live on Mamet alone.

Jerry: I thought you'd stick with me. No matter how much money I make.

Girlfriend: What money? There isn't any. Money's important, Jerry.

Jerry: Oh, man, why do you have to be so *Jewish*?

Girlfriend: I'm not being Jewish.

Jerry: You are.

Girlfriend: I'm not.

Jerry: You are.

Girlfriend: I'm not.

Jerry: You are.

Girlfriend: All right, I'm a Jew, okay?

Jerry: You're not.

Girlfriend: Yes I am.

Jerry: You're not.

Girlfriend: I am.

Jerry: Really, you're not.

Girlfriend: I went to synagogue sometimes as a kid. I'm a Jew. I'm a Jew. I'm a Jew.

Jerry: So what—

Girlfriend: What's a Jew?

Jerry: You tell me.

Girlfriend: I'm snot, I'm swill. *(Pause.)* There, it happened again. We're arguing in Mamet-style rhythm. And the substance of our argument is straight out of one of his essays. I never knew how impressionable I was.

Jerry: Don't get down on yourself. You're from a very accomplished race.

Girlfriend: When I grew up, Jewish meant only that you were onto Cary Grant's secret that he was a Jew. *(She hits herself on the forehead, clownishly.)* Oh, God, yes, it's Mamet again.

Girlfriend: You're succeeding, Jerry. My personality is being canceled and reconstituted along the lines devised by David Mamet.

    (Disgusted.) You want me to be something out of *Glengarry Glen Ross,* or *American Buffalo,* you pussy.

Jerry: You're the pussy.

Girlfriend: I'm not.

Jerry: You are.

Girlfriend: There we go again. Mamet-style. It's pathetic.

Jerry: What's wrong? Did you read something that you have a question about?

Girlfriend: You're a fossil. A male-chauvinist pig. It's all been brought out by him.

Jerry: I like it when you say "pussy". Say it again, will you?

Girlfriend: I'm not doing anything to further cement our relationship.

Jerry: What's gotten into you? Profanity—is liberating.

Girlfriend: I don't agree with your theory—or *Mamet's* theory. Obscenities are ugly. They're supposed to be powerful levers? To help us release our anger? Spare me.

Jerry: *(Rapture seizes him.)* I need you to talk filth to me. Link me with the universal angst that eats at us all.

The Girlfriend *decides to humor him.*

Girlfriend: You want to be linked? You piss-ant. Prick.

Jerry: Yes, please, more.

Girlfriend: Boobs. Tomato juice.

Jerry *(Momentarily in anguish.)* Tomato juice?

Girlfriend: *(Shrugs.)* I'm thirsty.

Jerry: What about me?

Girlfriend: It's always about you. Scrotum. Nipples.

Jerry: Scrotum, nipples. That's not obscene enough. I want words that are not words, but pure forms of energy.

Girlfriend: Fucked-up.

Jerry: Yes! Exactly!

Girlfriend: Penis.

Jerry: No. Not real anatomy.

Girlfriend: Cock, okay? Balls.

Jerry: Yes. Jerk-off!

The Girlfriend *flips out.*

Girlfriend: It's disgusting! You know what you are?

Jerry: I'm a buffalo. As strong as a Chicago American bull.

He snorts proudly a few times.

Girlfriend: Oh, Christ. *(She gets teary.)* You're a bastard. A bastard, Jerry. A bastard. Bastard. Bastard. *(She breaks down in tears.)* Bastard! Bastard! *(She sobs.* Jerry *recovers finally from his state of rapture to pay attention to her.)*

Jerry: That's the spirit. Don't you feel better now? Isn't it *cathartic?*

Girlfriend: No—fuck you.

Jerry: Fuck you.

Girlfriend: I said, *fuck you.*

The Girlfriend *stops crying.*

Jerry: It's true—we do talk an awful like characters in Mamet's plays. Why can't we talk smoother—like some of the characters in his movies?

Girlfriend: How about just being ourselves? *(Pause.)* If only you could be a fan of somebody more mature than David Mamet. Sure, the world's not perfect. But do you have to get into a writer that rubs our nose in it?

Jerry: You're directly criticizing Mamet?

Girlfriend: I am.

Jerry: That's not fair. You yourself talked like Mamet on our first date.

Girlfriend: I was trying to impress you by appearing macho. Independent, you know? Later I recognized those were Mamet-style lines. I should never have tried to get close to you that way.

I believe you once loved me. It's hard to know though—since your infatuation with the work of David Mamet started soon after our relationship began. I regret I brought back that book of his from the library that afternoon. Of course he's written so much you just had to leave your job and get into his whole oeuvre. I may have yielded and let you move in with me. But you'll never father a child of mine.

Jerry: *(Smiling, with fond memories.)* Oleanna. My first real book. But then we saw a play of his *live.*

Girlfriend: *(Sarcastically.)* And that was sheer fantasy-extravaganza-dee-lish.

Jerry: No. It was so authentic I almost shit.

Girlfriend: The sagas of ethnic urbanites turn you on, Jerry.

Jerry: Come on, let's rent a film of his.

Girlfriend: Martin Scorcese makes better films.

Jerry: He makes *different* films from David, that's all.

Girlfriend: If Scorcese wrote plays they'd be better than Mamet's.

Jerry: Do you have a sexual interest in Martin Scorcese or what? *(He picks up a book of a Mamet play. He opens to a page. He repeatedly points to it during his following speech.)* Listen: We live in a godless, chaotic city. Laws are of no use. Only the individual can keep himself in line. The going is rough. We take anxious steps to reach out to our fellow beings, hoping to establish trust as a bulwark against the rapid and relentless incursions of chance.

Yet trust is short-lived; the failure to get a fix on trust is crushing for us. We retreat into our clandestine worlds where we act selfishly. Where the Light eludes us. Yes, the world is cold; so cold we give up the Search for Meaning. All we have left is a scream in the dark. It is the tragic howl of the David Mamet Syndrome. This is our life! It's in all of Mamet's work. Not in Scorcese's. Now tell me who the genius is!

Girlfriend: It's you, Jerry. You've taken one minute to express what David Mamet's been trying to say his whole life. *(Pause.)* Look, I've got to go to the kitchen.

The marching drum music, like that at the top of the play, is heard. Jerry puts down the book he has been holding. The Girlfriend walks around in a large, loose circular way. If any props need to be moved for the next scene they should be now. Jerry keeps his distance from the Girlfriend—or any stagehands—should they walk on to assist the Girlfriend with the props.

B

The drum music stops. The Girlfriend picks up a glass of water that is on a table.

Girlfriend: I've just walked into the kitchen to mix myself a glass of iced tea. *(She puts the spoon in her glass and stirs. She takes a sip.)*

Stirring, stirring, now it is spurring:
There is one foe; his name's not Jim or Joe.
Stirring, spurring, my heart and mind concurring:
There is one factor,
And it's not the author, poet, playwright and ex-actor,
Raised in Chicago.
It's the beast next to me,
To him I've sacrificed my femininity,
It's blurring, blurring;
Stirring, stirring. Stirring, stirring.
Beside him I've become boyish, and a toy;
I must rise up and attack
To get my female purpose back.

Jerry *approaches her.*

Girlfriend: Why are you following me?

Jerry: David Mamet...

Girlfriend: You never leave this apartment. There is something called the out-of-doors.

Jerry: The air is polluted.

Girlfriend: Do something about it.

Jerry: I don't know that David is doing anything about it. He's got his hands full with other things. Hey, it's a highly specialized world. We can't all be presidents of the Sierra Club, or Greenpeace, as they call it in England. You know the English really like him. Over there they have problems with releasing their anger. They look to him.

Girlfriend: To release their anger?

Jerry: That's what I said. He's a *god* there. They'll always be angry. It's in the culture. The monarchy. The jealousy. The lack of tropical territory.

Girlfriend: Hong Kong—

Jerry: Hong Kong is finished. Given back to the Chinese. So in England things have gotten that much worse. *(Pause.)* Remember in the *Spanish Prisoner* where *(The* Girlfriend *tunes out.)* Joe drinks among the palm trees? ...You're not listening to me.

Girlfriend: I want another relationship. *(Pause.)* Have you ever listened to your dreams?

Jerry: I don't remember my dreams.

Girlfriend: That's why you need Mamet. It's a pity you have fictions instead of fantasies.

Jerry: They're one and the same.

Girlfriend: Dreams are said with poetry.

Jerry: David writes poetry. We've read *The Hero Pony* together.

Girlfriend: Maybe he should write a silent movie.

Pause.

Jerry: What do you mean?

Girlfriend: He should cut his losses. I don't believe he has a way with words.

Jerry: Ho! *(He holds up his hand, signaling her to stop.)* Did I hear you correctly? What'd you just say?

Girlfriend: The more Mamet I see, the more I believe he's a fraud.

Jerry: I can't believe you just said that!

Girlfriend: He's a recipe. There's no beautiful process. The tyranny of reason in the west, that's what John Ralston Saul calls it. Look at Mamet, where's the spontaneity?

Jerry: That's for the avant-garde. David Mamet hates the avant-garde.

Girlfriend: He's chop-chop, this bounces off that, tit for tat. That's the mechanics. Who cares? He gets paid for what he writes. It doesn't mean he's good at it.

Jerry: Ho! *(He holds his hand up to signal for her to stop speaking.)* Ho! Ho! You told me you loved *The Duck Variations*.

Girlfriend: I've changed my mind. They don't wear well over time. It's all Mamet-speak, it's not real poetry.

Jerry: That's right. Get the anger out, the *rage*. You want to lie down? Or you want to talk more?

Girlfriend: Yeah, chop-chop. Yak-yak.

Jerry: It's one thing dealing with your hostility, but you're being sadly reductive about his style.

Girlfriend: Yak-yak. Chop-chop. To distract you from his jumbled ideas.

Jerry: It's only yakking and chopping in so far that it's supposed to point up the ridiculousness of life.

Girlfriend: Mamet is ridiculous.

Jerry: The ridiculous *truth*.

Girlfriend: Whatever.

Jerry: The truth *is* ridiculous.

Girlfriend: You said the works of Mamet sum up our life.

Jerry: Uh huh.

Girlfriend: Then our life is ridiculous?

Jerry: Yes.

Girlfriend: Oh. Doesn't life matter to you, Jerry?

Jerry: I never said that.

Girlfriend: What are you saying, Jerry? Say what you *feel*, Jerry.

Jerry: *(Off in his own head space.)* David Mamet is greater than the Disney Company. He will write in all forms.

Girlfriend: I can't wait till he writes for ballet.

Jerry: David Mamet's trademark is one of abject frankness, whereas all college professors, politicians and comedians can only pretend integrity. David Mamet bestows authenticity upon all who are interested. Meanwhile, the great Russian, Stanislavsky, Mamet's personal god, hovers overhead, smiling benevolently in approval as David's work manifests itself as being both supremely realistic and deep.

Girlfriend: Like I said, let him do a dance piece.

Jerry: You still have an obsession about being a ballerina.

Girlfriend: It was a girlish fantasy.

Jerry: He'll write a ballet, you just watch.

Girlfriend: He won't. Want to know why?—Mozart. I read it the other day. He said he didn't like Mozart. And it's only Mozart who composed the greatest theater work that's ever been created. *Don Giovanni*—yeah, it's an opera. But Mamet's too crude to appreciate such a form. At least the words of *Don Giovanni* were written by a fellow Jew, maybe he can get into *that* dimension of it.

Jerry: A Jewish person wrote the words?

Girlfriend: DaPonte.

Jerry: Doesn't sound Jewish.

Girlfriend: It isn't. He took a Christian name to make life a little easier.

Jerry: He should've keep his name. Retained his identity.

Girlfriend: It's easy for you to say, not being Jewish.

Jerry: I wish I was Jewish so I could understand Mamet even more deeply. *(Pause.)* What David does is communicate far better than anyone has since the Declaration of Independence was written more than two hundred years ago.

Pause. The Girlfriend *ignores him. She takes out a bag of flour and mixes it with water in a bowl.*

Jerry: What are you doing?

Girlfriend: Something.

She continues to stir and mess around with the flour and water.

Jerry: But what's it going to be?

Girlfriend: I don't know.

Jerry: What do you mean, you don't know?

Girlfriend: Don't ask me what I *mean*. You heard me.

Jerry: I heard you say you don't know.

Girlfriend: That's what I said, Jerry.

Jerry: Don't *Jerry* me.

Girlfriend: You heard me. Then you asked me what I *meant!* I already told you. Wasn't it clear? You're just trying to expand our conversation. It was said once, why say it again? Boy, have you learned from Master Dave himself!

Jerry: You said "you don't know", when I asked you "what you were doing".

Girlfriend: That's not what you said exactly.

Jerry: Okay, I said, "What's it going to be?"

Girlfriend: Right. You must be so happy with yourself. Now we're right back where we started a minute ago. In true Mamet style.

Pause.

Jerry: What are you making?

Girlfriend: *(Trying to contain herself.)* A mess, maybe.

Jerry: Don't you have anything in mind?

Girlfriend: *(Still trying to contain herself.)* No.

Jerry: Then why are you doing it?

Girlfriend: Leave me alone. Go shave.

Jerry *stands watching his Girlfriend. She stops stirring the ingredients. She sets down the spoon and plunges her hands into the mixture and works it through her fingers)*

Jerry: David Mamet prefers rock music over classical music. That's why he married a rock singer, not a violinist.

Girlfriend: At least he made a commitment to someone before he destroyed her career.

Jerry: He can always get divorced if he doesn't like her.

Girlfriend: I don't want to talk about her or him.

Jerry: You admitted their song, *Primitive Man* is great.

Girlfriend *(In a mocking voice, being "serious".)* "Our western world is devolving into a more primitive, more effective society."

Jerry: Yes! The song hints at it. Only his essay spells it out. Very clever, the interplay between his theory and practice.

Girlfriend: *(Sarcastically.)* Yeah, pro-found. *(Pause. She continues to play in the dough while she recites:)*
"Weep not, child,
Weep not, my darling,
With these kisses let me remove your tears,
The ravening clouds shall not long be victorious,
They shall not long possess the sky, they devour the
stars only in apparition,
Jupiter shall emerge, be patient, watch again another
night, the Pleiades shall emerge,
They are immortal, all those stars both silvery and golden
shall shine out again,
The great stars and the little ones shall shine out again,
they endure,
The vast immortal suns and the long-enduring pensive
moons shall again shine."

Jerry: What's that?

Girlfriend: Something from the library.

Jerry: Who wrote it?

Girlfriend: David Mamet.

Jerry: I don't remember that poem.

Girlfriend: The poem's a poem by Walt Whitman.

Jerry: Why are you messing with my head?

Girlfriend: I miss the library.

Jerry: So, do you think you'll give them a call?

Pause.

Girlfriend: Yeah, I'd like to work there again. Stop pressuring me.

Jerry: I'm not.

Girlfriend: You are. *(Pause.)* Hey, how come Mamet doesn't he ever write about the sky?

Jerry: I think he does.

Girlfriend: Where?

Jerry: I don't know right off hand.

Girlfriend: Why don't you look in one of your Mamet books?

Jerry: Not right now.

Girlfriend: Usually we're surrounded by about forty percent of sky at any given time.

Jerry: Not in the city. Not indoors. My place, modern man's place, is indoors. It's where the tension is. It's where we need David's battering-ram. To split open walls, knock down doors. Spray words like bullets.

Girlfriend: That's too much like combat for me.

Jerry: Have you ever been in combat?

Girlfriend: You're right, Jerry, I haven't. But *we're* ready for combat, aren't we? You've got a gun. And you're a member of the National Rifle Association. All because of Mamet. He brags about belonging to the N.R.A.—and the American Civil Liberties Union! To most people, two very contrasting organizations, but to a Mametophile, totally in harmony.

But Jerry, you haven't joined the A.C.L.U. What's the problem? I thought you were trying to cultivate the image of being complicated—like your hero. Let me help you on your way. I'll call them. *(She cleans herself up and goes to the phone. She picks it up, dials telephone information and says into the phone:)* The American Civil Liberties Union, please.

Jerry: We don't have the money to join.

Girlfriend: *(Into the phone.)* Thank you. *(She listens to the number, memorizes it, then hangs up and dials again. As she is dialing, she says to* Jerry:*)* Money, yeah. Maybe I have my own reasons. *(Her call is answered. She speaks into the phone.)* Hello, A.C.L.U.? I need to know if there's someone on your staff that could take a case that involves stress. *(Pause)* Yes, I'll try to be more particular. A case involving the power of the word—verbal suggestion, you know? *(Pause)* You don't understand? *(Pause.)* Everyone's away fighting for justice. *(Pause.)* I'm aware you only take special cases. Why do you think I'm calling? Look, you've defended people whose mental health has been undermined by *sickly factors in our society.* *(Long pause.)* I'm talking about provocation, and you want to talk to me about Plato's Republic? When can I call to talk a real person, not a college intern? *(Pause.)* Okay, bye.

She hangs up the phone.

Jerry: You're angry.

Girlfriend: No.

Jerry: Anger. See, everybody has it. I had it when I was a dentist. *(Sighing contentedly.)* Ah, I like this life. Free from the daily torture of being a tooth-puller.

Girlfriend: Imagine how they felt in the chair. *(Pause.)* Life was rough at a hundred dollars an hour.

Jerry: Those lawsuits. Some guy wanted to shake me down, saying that I bumped him as I swung the drill over. And he was permanently brain damaged? Yep, someone perceives you're on top and they just want to bring you down.

Girlfriend: Jerry, don't mind the mess. *(She mutters to herself.)* You won't.

She starts to leave.

Jerry: Where you going?

Girlfriend: To the bedroom.

Jerry: To lie down?

Girlfriend: I don't know.

Jerry: You're damned indecisive lately.

Girlfriend: I'm working on that.

The drum marching music is heard. Again, the Girlfriend walks around in a large, loose, circular way. If any props need to be moved for the next scene they should be now. Jerry keeps his distance.

C

The drumming ends.

Girlfriend: Just walking into the bedroom. *(She goes to a closet and brings out a rifle. She starts to clean the rifle—among other things, she pushes a wire with a felt tip down the barrel of the gun. Jerry keeps his distance while she works on the gun; he does not look at her.)* No one can play innocent to the fact that a gun is manufactured to kill. All other arguments to the otherwise are not honest. Like... self-defense? In today's world? Who's kidding who? A bandit or an army is not going to bust through my door, and if they did, I wouldn't be ready with my rifle in time to fend them off. No, what we have here is a terrible machine, lending great power to whoever holds it. No wonder it's the favorite instrument of those who feel weak inside.

What I can't comprehend, but then of course the world's not a logical place, is that people fear death but they don't always make that connection between death and guns. How come we have so many guns in our country? You don't rake or hoe with a gun. You don't balance your checkbook with it. You load it and you shoot somebody dead. Or at least you're able to capitalize on a person's fear of being dead. So you threaten them and they turn over their property, their secrets, their sex... some useful information, perhaps. Then you've successfully changed the course of life to fit your will.

> Everyone knows if the gun goes off
> Bullets'll have little time to tear the air.
> > If there is *any* time, though,
> > It's spent begging the god behind the gun
> > To please, take something, anything,
> > Only leave me with as much life
> > As thou, sweet god, canst possibly can.

If you use the gun on yourself, you instantly change the course of *your* life—some say it's within your moral rights to do that.

Jerry *comes over to her.*

Jerry: What are you doing?

Girlfriend: I'm cleaning your rifle.

Jerry: Why?

Girlfriend: It might need it.

Jerry: Might?

Girlfriend: It might. Who knows.

Jerry: Who knows.

Girlfriend: Didn't I just say that?

Jerry: Why clean it now?

Girlfriend: *(She cannot answer "To kill somebody." She speaks to herself.)* No, I couldn't bring myself to do it.

Jerry: I bet he's a fine deer hunter.

Girlfriend: Who?

Jerry: David Mamet.

Girlfriend: *(To herself.)* Well, maybe I could—

Jerry: I've been thinking I should start acting. You know, to get closer to his frame of mind. He was an actor. Then he started writing.

Girlfriend: Fascinating. *(Pause. She continues to clean the gun.)* Seems no matter where I go around here it all comes back to the same thing.

Jerry: What's that?

Girlfriend: We don't talk about the things we used to. You know, *before*?

Jerry: Before what?

Girlfriend: Before, Jerry. Before.

Jerry: What do you mean, before?

Girlfriend: Don't ask me what I mean. You know, before.

Jerry: I don't know.

Girlfriend: Before? Before *him?*

Jerry: Him?

Girlfriend: Come on, Jerry. He's radically transformed our lives. I wonder what I ever saw in you.

Jerry: You were going to come in here and lie down, I thought. I appreciate you looking after my gun but you really should relax.

Girlfriend: How can I relax?

Jerry: I just told you, lie down.

Girlfriend: I don't want to. It'll only make me angry.

Jerry: I love that word. The concept of it. It has so many dramatic repercussions.

Girlfriend: There are other dramatic possibilities in the world, Jerry. Why does drama have to be so obsessed with male characters who need to work out their rage? Can't drama be touching, soft, and wonderful?

Jerry: Don't look to David Mamet for that. Even though he says his aim is to entertain, don't be fooled. There's not one thing he's ever written that's any fun at all.

Girlfriend: I know.

Jerry: But that's the point.

The Girlfriend *picks up a rag and shines the gun.*

Girlfriend: Isn't there anything else that interests you? Rather than...

Jerry: What?

Girlfriend: I can't say his name anymore. I may not be here some day. *(Pause.)* I hope, for your sake, that you can disengage from this small, vacuum-world that you've gotten yourself into. I'm trying, I feel compassion for you, while at the same time I'm fighting the most horrible, distressing thoughts I've ever had in my life. You may say it's only a momentary dramatic crisis. But anger's not a passing storm. It's disturbing, truly disturbing. Anger makes you want to do real things, very real things that are dangerous. Dangerous to oneself and others. *(She throws down the rag in her hand. She picks up a few bullets. She loads them in the gun.)* I don't want to have to *force* a separation between you and your vacuum-world, and you and me. I don't want to use a machine, Jerry, to make you listen.

Jerry *picks up a book nearby—it is by Mamet. He reads from it.*

Jerry: "You really are just a bitch, aren't you? You fucking twat."

Girlfriend: Those are fighting words, Jerry.

She cocks the gun. Jerry *is unfazed. He thinks she is "just" wrestling with her anger. He continues to dig the Mamet book.*

Jerry: *(Still reading.)* "What are you doing?" *(Pause.)* "Ah, sit on my face." *(His* Girlfriend *cocks the gun a second time.)* "Dumb dickhead."

Girlfriend: Is this the way you're going to talk me down from a psychotic high, Jerry?

Jerry: *(Still reading.)* "Stupid cocksucker." *(Pause. He turns away from the book to respond her.)* I'm your boyfriend, not a shrink.

Girlfriend: You were a dentist once. Have a look at this cavity. *(She raises the gun against him, he smiles. He does not take her seriously. She moves the gun up to his mouth and puts it inside it.)* I'm leaving you Jerry. I suppose I do care that you would pollute the world with your idolatry over that you-know-who. I've got nothing against writers, per se, after all, I'm a librarian. It's just you, Jerry. You're a scumbag. Not all men are scumbags but you certainly are. (Jerry *tries to say something but he cannot because the gun barrel is in his mouth.)* What are you saying, you fuckhead?

She moves the gun slightly out of his mouth to let him speak.

Jerry: I love it, I love it. It's perfect Mamet!

She rams the gun back into his mouth. She nonchalantly reaches down and depresses the trigger of the gun. It goes off and Jerry falls dead to the ground.

Girlfriend: You asshole. You'll never do that again. Thank you for giving me the necessary instrument to go on with my life. *(She throws the rifle at Jerry's corpse.)* I guess I should thank David Mamet, though. Yes, I've said his name. I should thank David for joining the National Rifle Association and influencing you to buy a gun. *(She pulls herself together and goes over to the phone. She picks it up and dials. Her call is answered. She speaks into the phone)* Hello? Hello. Yes, I've spoken to you before. Are there any actual lawyers there? *(Pause.)* They're off fighting for justice. *(Pause.)* Sorry for that crack about interns. *(Pause.)* As I remember one of Plato's arguments in the Republic ran along the lines that life can imitate art. And that bad art can make us do bad things. *(Pause.)* Well, yeah, I have the most incredible case for you. My tale is really to long to tell in one short conversation. I would imagine I'll see you soon enough at the office. *(Pause.)* Excuse me, my throat's getting dry, I've got to hang up now. *(Pause.)* It was nice talking to *you. (Pause.)* Bye.

She leaves the bedroom. There is no music.

D

The Girlfriend *goes into the kitchen and pours herself a glass of water. She looks down at the messy dough and does nothing about it. She looks out into space.* Jerry *gets up off the ground, dusts himself off, and goes over to his* Girlfriend. *She does not look at him, she may still hear him but she could care less what he is saying.*

Jerry: The opinion of the world is divided over Mamet. I'm aware of that. I recognize him as more than a nation-builder. He's an inspired prophet. Other people think he's just crap. They're wrong. *He's* the one that's popular. Even if he hits a slump his star will rise again and take its place in the heavens for eternity. For he teaches what no teacher can teach and what no acting coach can coach.

Yes, I am an stage actor. I prize every word that David Mamet writes or speaks, and that means his acting theory—which is *better* than Stanislavsky's. Mamet is a pyramid that *all* humans should climb. No matter what walk of life. On the way up that pyramid, we will find fury, and associative language—as Northrop Frye calls it. But once we're through the eye of the needle, then we've unlocked natural expression for everyone. In the theater and elsewhere.

As for my girlfriend... *(He gestures to the* Girlfriend.) We all know by now, she's a junior player in all this. But that's the way it is on this planet. Get used to it. Someday

Mamet may see it differently, he may get in touch with his feminine side and create female characters of lasting quality. But that'll never change the fact that my girlfriend was unable to come to terms—like most people—with their anger. And that she had to blame somebody else and be dramatic about it. And that she went ahead and used a commonly available stage prop to do her cheap parlor trick.

Oh, well. I'm not *really* an intellectual like David. I will say though, that as life imitates art, art imitates art, and never shall the twain meet unless we achieve it with Mr. Mamet's help. I hope you think I've done a pretty good job—how true was I? Tell me that I'm being real. That *would* please me. *(Pause.)*

I thank you *sincerely* for your time. (Jerry *raises his hands and applauds the audience, then stops.)* Oh. *(He farts.)* That baby's been trying to squeeze its way out the whole time I've been up here. But it's okay. Mamet would say if you do it naturally there's never a false moment. *(He farts again. Defensively.)* I'm not supposed to apologize for farting.

The parade marching music fades up. The brass instruments enter into the music, the whole ensemble plays while Jerry *and his* Girlfriend *stand on their marks. Soon the music fades as the lights fade to black and the play ends.*

More, For the Art of It

Traditional modern science aims to get at the truth by being rational, objective and thorough. Art should not be thorough, it should not fill in blanks. Some blanks must be left open for the audience themselves to fill.

Though a journalist armed with facts may seek to arouse identification, provoke a small discovery, stimulate some pity and fear within us with his or her story, the range of results a journalist seeks is narrow compared to the range sought by a theater-writer who aims for truth via powerful "unstable", or variable images. An artist may at times make use of journalistic fact—but if he or she over-indulges the journalistic manner (it is only a manner), art is hindered.

We hear that art is supposed to hold a mirror up to life, to nature, to the human condition. This metaphor of the mirror is problematic—I ask, what *kind* of mirror are talking about? Not made of glass or metal, an artistic "mirror" gives us invented images that show some kind of concern about (or for) the human condition. Relationships involving money, love, safety, solidarity, what-have-you, are first worried over by the dramatist and finally by the audience. There is no "unbiased" mirror possible in the process of art. In fact, the "mirror" is grossly distorted at times to point up certain themes and problems with humans and their society.

It seems to me that in theater improvisation is overrated. Theater is, among other things, storytelling and debate (whether the debate is self-contained in the play or not); good theater carefully indulges in selected symbols, it weaves them and story-matter in surprising, uncommon ways; at last the actor presents the work face-to-face, to the spectator. The symbolic element of art takes a good deal of poetic ability—and time—to work out in order for it to be effective. The catch is that art must possess spontaneity but it cannot be for the most part improvised—as if improvisation were a guarantee of spontaneity anyway.

Many plays might be made up of arresting character or story ideas, yet they are weak in language. Theater, as an *art*, is special, different, separate from everyday life and it can demonstrate this in its use of language. The only way a play that is filled with everyday language can step away from the brink of "no art" is for it to use other means that break with Naturalism. Thornton Wilder's *Our Town* is just such a play. Though its language is often mundane, the play has its inventions. The battle against excessive realism in American Theater has been going for many decades. Recently Arthur Miller (who like Wilder, looks to other means instead of heightened language to make his art) discusses his generation's struggles with it in *Harper's* (March 1999).

There is a connection between excessive realism in art and excessive materialism in society. Cold materialists reduce all art to entertainment. Their notion is that art is an intermission from work that ultimately leads all people back to work—hence art should be distracting and escapist; it should stir up no feelings that cannot be fixed by simply laughing, crying or feeling proud; when done to order, realism is priced competitively and can deliver "satisfactory" results, since the intellect and soul are of little concern.

Remarks Before the Remaining Plays

I have been asked by the playwright to introduce the remaining plays because he would like their connection to Japanese theater to be known. Though the playwright has been influenced in his break with Naturalism by several types of Japanese theater, he has mentioned traditional Noh theater as a highly important resource. Certainly the literature of Noh is a storehouse of works that demonstrate ingenious, wonderful and profound ways in which theater can be made; the Noh looms as a validating force for any playwright who imagines and writes for a theater of non-realism.

Noh theater is both lyrical and dramatic; it appears somewhat prescriptive in its dramatic form to the first-time viewer; it is capable of, and demands however, much in the way of invention on the part of the writer—for multi-skilled performers (with or without masks), choral members (who must chant and sing) and musicians must all eventually join to realize a drama that is, while not devoid of realistic elements, fundamentally symbolic and musical. A dream-like atmosphere hangs over the best of traditional Noh; the plays are plays of the spirit; the other-world lives within the bodies of those in the performance space; the otherworld can too almost be touched, since it is felt to be located immediately just off stage. It is not surprising that such a theater is "peopled" by travelers, monks, ghosts, spirits and figures proceeding to a final transformation. The setting of a traditional Noh drama is always a highly charged junction; the dramatic pay-off co-exists with the spiritual progress-to-an-end of the main character, played by the principle performer—the *shite*.

Most theater uses surprise and suspense in its storytelling; Noh is no exception, but in contrast to Naturalistic theater, the surprise and suspense is "worked into" a theatrical fabric that includes song, music, dance and gesture. Whereas the drama of Naturalism relies on escalating psychological conflict for its structure and ultimate effects, traditional Noh commits itself to organization and elaboration according to the natural, organic rhythm of *jo-ha-kyu*—*jo* means "beginning" or "opening"; *ha* means "break" or "development," and *kyu* gives the sense of "fast" or "climax". Thus, the *rhythm* of Noh, with long-range notions of *jo-ha-kyu* down to smaller manifestations of *jo-ha-kyu*, further helps to make this Japanese performing art form an entirely different theater experience than something that can be found in the West.°°

The gentle surrealism and the musical qualities of *Jesus and the Monkfish* disarm the spectator who wants to learn more, in a realistic sense, about the characters of this play. At the heart of the piece is Carla's striving for something beyond the world she knows: in a word, happiness. However, there are spiritual considerations—and we find, spiritual and ethical *conditions* attached to her quest. Her story is told with glimpses of realism and at various junctures the play shows stylistic affinities with Western psychological drama. However, with the otherworldly figure of James, and the barrier-free physical setting of the beach, the music, and the repetitive entrances of the male characters, *Jesus and the Monkfish* goes its own way in setting up a theatrical world of considerable freedom. The real and everyday "facts" of Carla's predicament, and her journey away from it, are thus able to be presented in a selective manner. This manner is seized upon and exploited for its poetic potentialities by the dramatist.

The playwright credits a production, brought to New York from the countryside of Japan, as having a powerful formal influence upon the writing of *Behave, My Sorrow.* However rewarding it may have been to see the performances presented by the masters of Awaji Island, Tait, with his good knowledge of theater gained beforehand, certainly brought much himself to his first encounter with ritual puppetry. After seeing the performance he must have sensed himself capable of writing speech in a dialogue form that drives the spectator's attention relentlessly forward.

The play is riotously funny though a profoundly gentle respect for human character and its weaknesses underpins the fantasy. From a woman concerned about implications of a conversion to communism, we hear: "But will I be compelled to march in parades?" Towards the play's end we see Bruno's comic "murder" of his partner; this suggests however that Bruno has finally become a true disciple of Buddy's religion, for now he himself is practicing the teaching of "walking away and forgetting."

The play's electronic music, lighting effects and scenic devices are a natural outgrowth of the on stage fantasy created by a single player with a hand puppet. The parent-to-child poem that precedes the play's final two lines of verse layers still another voice into the play; the "catharsis/purification", and the last lines of the play, help to propel one's imagination far into poetic space at the drama's end.

With *Live Free or Die* the dramatist departs from the simplicity, yet technical sophistication of *Jesus and the Monkfish* and *Behave, My Sorrow*. At an elementary level, the play has commonalties with the other plays in this volume: an "open" setting, a disrupted linearity to its storytelling, symbolic characters mixed with a sense of the real, a combination of prose and poetry, etc. In the beginning of *Live Free or Die* there is a Pirandello-like "prelude", a situation that takes place before the rehearsal of the play that in fact we are just about to see. After the prelude, a chorus recites a kind of poetry and sings; we have the impression that this chorus will be the tale's real storyteller—the chorus introduces the main characters after which the actors leave the stage, never having said a word. However the role of storyteller for the chorus is soon abandoned; in this "bait and switch" operation we are left with the chorus' funeral dirge and processional song, "Bones, bones..." with variants to trouble us throughout the rest of the play—and beyond.

The enormous power of this play lies in its contrasts, sometimes even violent ones, that focus the spectator's attention. There is the realistic horror of American prison life, the calm and idealism of Zen. Unpredictable events converge upon us; we ask ourselves, why this event now?

In terms of language, there are contrasts between faux Elizabethan speech suitable to a Renaissance fair, realistic contemporary speech, the dialogue of non-Native speakers of English, words read from newspaper ads, words from jail reports, choral chants and songs.

Despite the initially incongruous and seemingly grotesque counterpoint between the scenes that make up *Live Free or Die*, the play on the whole shows a remarkable unity. I am reminded of the different scenic worlds of Kabuki theater clashing, as they do in the "mixed world" plays of Kabuki's so-called "decadent period". In the Kabuki plays, as well as in this, a rich spectrum of activity is indulged; the drama does not confine itself to one limited niche, restricted to stock characters and more or less predictable situations.

Of course the playwright is not looking to tell a "prison story" in linear fashion here; but during the first encounter with the drama it may be helpful for an audience member to think of certain scenes (fragments, episodes) as reenactments of "real" events from the prison story that supposedly underlies the play. These fragments may not necessarily be in the chronological order suggested by various clues in the drama. The hero's wounding (page 263) occurs in a mock medieval joust ("ordeal"?) But the "swooning" that is part of this (one of several dreams in an outdoor setting that formally may recall scenes in *Midsummer Night's Dream*) could also be understood as a fantasy version of a "real" knife wounding in a prison brawl and the feverish dreams that follow as he lay recovering. There are many beautifully open questions to the play but the multitudes of people in prison today serving mandatory sentences for drug related offenses is a reality—a social reality—for all of us. Regarding the fictional William of the play, I believe he is *spiritually* free in the end, or to phrase it more cautiously perhaps, he has finally become acquainted with the steps to take to make himself free. A comment at the play's end helps us grasp what is going on. "Flags Man: Very weird. *(To the Actress.)* Is he in prison? Or what? Actress: Ask him. Flags Man: It's obvious he doesn't know..." Prison is a multipurpose metaphor.

Surely the playwright wants us to respond, each in our own ways, to what "big issue" is in play. For me the play is a Buddhist teaching or parable on how one can be free from suffering. In the play the enigma is resolved *after* the point where William understands the significance of a momentary interruption—a cold and very brief factual report of physical violence in prison—to a lengthy quotation about the calm and supportive aesthetics of the Japanese tea ceremony. In a quieter mood and in the persona of William, Tait also proceeds to address his idea of theater aesthetics by reworking a description from the previous tea ceremony narrative of how tea utensils—objects—are placed in space, how they are arranged and organized. William/the playwright address the chorus, thanking them for "being my thoughts..." and adds: "It's the arrangement of things that will help me through." Fairly heady stuff; nonetheless the playwright also succeeds on a *sensual* plane in creating a brilliant, organic play out of seemingly idiosyncratic fragments, out of what might be termed in a new sense appropriate for this play "mixed worlds." Here is the real reason why *Live Free or Die* is able to instruct, entertain and solace those of us, the spectators, who also need—each one of us—to live free *before* dying.

Frank Hoff
Toronto

°°*For those interested in more technical discussion of Noh, see the* Noh Performance Guide Series *(edited by Bethe, Emmert, et al.) and the splendid recent review concerning the series by Dr. Hoff in* Asian Theatre Journal, *Vol. 16, No. 1, Spring 1999, pp. 124-7.—L.T.*

Jesus and the Monkfish

The storytelling of *Jesus and the Monkfish* reminds me stylistically of the storytelling in films by Luis Buñuel and Jean Cocteau. However, at the time of writing the play I was reading Edna St. Vincent Millay's *Aria da Capo*, Waley's translation of Noh plays and Yukio Mishima's *Five Modern No Plays*.

Though Carla fights her sensual nature to find comfort in the cosmic, she is aware of the price she is paying. There is some nobility to her.

Music is almost a character in itself in the play.

A public reading of *Jesus and the Monkfish* directed by Michelle Powell was first presented by students at the ArtsFirst Festival, Harvard University, May 2, 1997. This play is dedicated to Joan and Walter Luikart.

The Characters

Carla   Female, late 20s, early 30s.

Frank   Male, 30s, at least two years older
                         than Carla.

James   Male, late 20s, early 30s.

Place: A sandy beach in Massachusetts.

Time: The present.

Jesus and the Monkfish

The Scene

On a sandy sea beach in Massachusetts. A hazy summer day. When the lights come up we see two beach chairs, a beach umbrella and a cooler for food and drinks. Carla, in a bathing suit, is seated in one of the chairs. After a minute Frank, in running shorts, enters jogging. From time to time as he talks to Carla *he runs in place.*

Frank: Muggy.

Carla: Don't jog then.

Frank: Maybe it's time for a beer.

Carla: I've been thinking, Frank.

Frank: Don't think. Relax. We're at the beach. *(Pause.)* I'm not ready for a beer yet. 'Cause they're not cold. Because you forgot to put them in the ice. When we left home.

Carla: I've been thinking that there are a lot of people like you—unthinking people. They sure expect a lot from people like me.

Frank *spots his baseball cap near the cooler. He picks it up and puts it on his head. He starts to leave.*

Frank: Cold beer. The way to my heart. You screwed it up again.

He jogs off. Carla *is left alone in her beach chair. She bursts into tears, then tries to relax in her chair. She cannot. She stops crying. She closes her eyes.* James *enters, dressed in a short-sleeve white dress shirt, open at the collar, and slacks. He has the composure of an Indian swami. He approaches* Carla, *looks at her with compassion. She senses someone is nearby. She opens her eyes and looks up, startled.*

James: Have I startled you?

Carla: Where'd you come from?

James: The fff— ...the road.

Carla: What road? *(Pause.)*

James: Carla.

Carla: How do you know my name? (James *is silent.*) You're not from around here.

James: I've come to give you back your key. (Carla *is confused. Pause.*) The key to your heart.

Carla: *(Brushing him off.)* Well, okay, goodbye.

James: You don't need to push me away. Relegate me to a high shelf. Like the shelf where you've stuck that old dish of potpourri.

Carla: You've been in my bedroom?

James: My feet are hot. They could do with a rinse. *(Pause.)*

Carla: Where did you come by your information? My potpourri?

James: I'm sort of a neighbor. (*Pause. They look at one another.*)

Carla: Jesus said, "You should love your neighbor as yourself."

James: Something like that.

Carla *sighs. Pause. She sizes* James *up.*

Carla: Understand that I'm being considerate of you because I'm a Christian. Are you thirsty? (*She gestures to the cooler in the sand.*)

James: No.

Carla: Hungry?

James: I don't eat much anymore. Food isn't what keeps me going these days.

Carla, *trusting* James, *recognizes something about him—something perhaps god-like. She gasps. Then:*

Carla: There's another kind of sustenance.

James: Of course.

Carla: (*She gestures to him to sit down.*) Make yourself at home.

James: There are those who wait for someone. To help them create a home. (*Pause.*) You've been upset.

Carla: Jesus said, "Blessed is the one who doesn't lose faith in me."

James: That he did.

Carla: I'm not doing so good today. Frank treats me badly.

James: Your brother's a selfish man, isn't he? *(She does not want to admit this.)* But people aren't all bad, right?

Carla: *(With conviction.)* That's right. *(Pause.)* He orders me around. Then he tells me I can't stand on my own two feet. I lean on religion he says.

James: He doesn't realize how pure and simple your faith is.

Carla: I moved in with him. Only after I quit my job. I kind of cook and clean.

James: You have time on your hands. Would you like to go out to the forest with me?

Carla: The forest? You mean, for a walk? *(Pause.)* On a date? *(Pause.)* I have to think about it.

James: Don't think about it too long. Or you could wind up marrying Frank.

Carla: Marrying Frank? He's my brother!

James: There's a bond between you two.

Carla: *(Surprisingly candid.)* Just a hefty knot.

James: How about it?

Carla: Going out? I don't know you.

James: You can get to know me. Like I know you. Out in the forest.

Carla: We don't need a forest. *(Pause.)* I have to watch myself. I'm too trusting. I don't believe in pre-marital sex. I'm a Christian now.

James: There's another side though. Your needs.

Carla *stares at him. She thinks something over.*

Carla: I know who you are now!

James: Yes?

Carla: I do. *(She laughs in a moment of sad recognition.)* Yes! Yes. You're the devil! (James *is disappointed. Pause.)* You're not?

James: No.

Pause. She wants to believe him.

Carla: Do you believe that God so loved the world that he gave his only son, so that we can repent our sins and have everlasting life?

James: You are lonely.

Carla: *(Tersely.)* I know what desires are about. I was married once. So there.

James: Jesus is your new husband. *(Pause.)* What can I do? To make you feel safe enough to go with me?

Carla: That's what the devil does. He always goes back to temptation. I wasn't sure the devil existed but now I'm sure.

James: You're sure I'm the devil?

Carla: Not really. *(She touches her head.)* I'm very warm.

Frank *enters jogging. At times, when he is not speaking, he will jog in place some.*

Frank: *(To* James.) Horning your way in here? Stay away from my sister. I can't turn my back for five minutes. This beach here, it's our spot.

James: You're gone a lot. At sea. I thought she might like the company.

Frank: I'm gone a lot? You'd better believe it. *(Proudly.)* I have to fish for a living. Long hours, hard work.

Carla: Frank, he doesn't want to hear your problems.

Frank: *(Looks out to the water.)* The ocean is practically fished out. Except for the monkfish. Them monkfish were shit fish my father's whole lifetime. Now, you take a monkfish. You cut off its fat tail. You sell it as a delicacy. A delicacy, what a joke!

Carla: Just be nice to him.

Frank: *(To James.)* As a matter of fact, I'm looking for investors. I need to buy some new equipment.

James: I don't believe money makes one happy.

Frank: *(Annoyed.)* I'm talking about survival. *(Pause.)* I didn't catch your name.

James: James. *(Pause. Frank wants to know more.)* ...Newcomb.

Frank: *(To Carla.)* This isn't that weird guy that used to ring in the middle of the night?

Carla: We may be going out together.

Frank: *(To James.)* Listen. Carla's all set. She's a subscriber. To magazines. (Frank *rolls his eyes.*) She's got an interest in theology.

Carla: He's asked me out to the forest.

Frank: Forest! Buddy, you've got a lot of nerve. *(Pause. Frank looks James over.)* You can't even take my sister out to *dinner.* Out to dance. Out for coffee. No, you want to jump her in the out of doors.

James: I've been searching. I stop because... I've found love.

Frank: Love?!

Carla: *(Elated.)* It's wonderful! *(She gets up out of her chair and goes over near* James.

James: I feel it throughout my whole being. *(To* Carla.) A little bird told me to come dressed in gold. I laughed. I said I didn't need to. You don't mind my clothes, do you?

She gazes at James. She is in love.

Carla: They're perfectly fine.

James: As I left, the tree was as still as the morning dew.

Frank: Did they unlock the doors to the mental hospital this afternoon?

James: *(To* Carla.) I said, "Sweet bird, rest quietly there, I'll bring you back a lock of her precious hair." *(He reaches out and gently brings his hand down through* Carla's *hair.)*

Frank: That does it! Out. Or I'm gonna get my rifle. Nobody touches her.

James *and* Carla *gaze at one another, on the brink of caressing each other.*

Frank: I'm gonna kill your ass.

James: Like you do the sharks in the sea?

Carla: I think I love this man, Frank.

Frank: *(To* James.) You probably got a police record as long as my arm.

James breaks his concentration with Carla.

James: You won't have to get your gun. I'm going soon.

Carla: *(Crestfallen.)* You just got here.

Frank: What's your hurry now? *(He thinks he has found the answer.)* He's got a drug addiction. He needs to go get his fix.

James: *(To* Carla.) I'd like you to have my phone number. Please call. When you're comfortable about seeing me. *(He writes his number on the paper and hands it to her. He then takes out his checkbook. To* Frank.) You question whether or not I'm genuinely in love with your sister. Since the only thing which makes an impression upon you is money, I'll give you, say, a hundred fifty thousand dollars. So you can upgrade your fishing business. Please, take this check as a sign of the seriousness of my intentions towards your sister. *(He writes out the check and hands it to* Frank. Frank *examines the check.)*

Frank: Ha, ha! Very funneee! Bouncy, bouncy. *(Pause.)* What do you take me for? I know what you take my sister for. I'll call the cops. Got you on something now. This check'll throw you right into the county jail.

James: The police'll find nothing wrong with my check.

Frank: Whatever you say, Jimbo.

Carla: Frank, I have a good feeling about James.

Frank: You had a good feeling about your husband. So good your marriage lasted a whole eight months.

Carla: James is different.

Frank: You only think so. *(He sticks the check into his shorts pocket.)*

Carla: He's serious.

James: I'll go now. I wish you every happiness. *(Seriously.)* Peace, joy, and love.

Frank: Thank you very much, Pope John Paul Mahatma Gandhi.

James: *(To* Carla.) You and I shall meet in our dreams tonight. You dream of a rippling brook. I'll dream of the forest. I'll bring the forest to your brook.

Frank: You won't ever get that close. *(To* James.) Carla lives the life of a monk, er, I mean nun, right now. It suits her all right.

Carla: I believe you are a good man, James. Are you a Christian? If you're not a Christian ...

James: Tonight. Bring your brook to my forest.

Frank: Get going.

Carla *smiles at* James *with hope.*

Carla: Don't go.

Frank: *(Bends down, and half whispers to her.)* Don't get emotional.

Carla: I believe I can be happy with him.

Frank: Believe? Let's get down to brass tacks. You're not the most attractive girl in the world. But you've got what men want. You know. And they want it bad. I'm trying to be delicate, here. *(Pause.)* I realize you want to get married again. But do you have to stop for every tomcat that comes to your milk bowl?

Carla: You're disgusting.

Pause. Suddenly James *extends his arms in front of himself, he crosses his arms and crosses them back, then thrusts his arms up in the air. Lights come on full force.*

Frank: *(Shielding his eyes from the brightness.)* Hey, what's with the sun? *(If Frank has been wearing sunglasses he takes them off and puts them on again.)*

Frank: What's going on? I'm blind. Help me, Carla, I'm blind!

Carla: *(Calmly.)* I can't see anything either.

Orchestral music. The musical passage gains in strength. One more light comes on. James *brings his arms back down to his side.*

James: Carla?

Carla: *(Still blinded, relieved.)* You're here.

Frank: *(Blinded, to* James.*)* You bastard.

James: No need to worry. We're in the forest.

The music gets softer in volume. Carla *shields her eyes.* Frank *continues to be incapacitated by the bright light.*

Carla: I can't see a thing.

James: You need time to adjust.

Frank: *(To* James.*)* If I could see, I'd smack you. *(He takes a few swings at* James, *but* James *is nowhere close to him.)*

James: This is where you slip down the garter.

Carla: The garter? The ...bride's garter?

James: Of course. Isn't the music fine?

The music continues.

Carla: It's beautiful.

James: Just as life should be.

Frank: I don't know what you're trying to do to us but it won't work.

James: You'll be back to your boat tomorrow. For now you ought to see the forest. *(Looking around.)* This is where I live.

Frank: I don't see no forest.

James: *(To Both.)* Can you see that tree over there?

Frank: What tree?

Carla: I'm beginning to see my hand in front of my face.

James: Good.

He goes over to Carla *and kisses her softly on the cheek. Pause. She is happy. She touches his arm in a warm manner. Frank snorts, as if he smells something.*

Frank: What's going on? What are you doing with my sister?

Carla: *(Smiling.)* This is the way day should be. *(Pause.)* Light like this cures depression. That's what they said in a magazine.

Carla: *(Eyes still opened only slightly.)* James, do you know what the firmament is?

James: I've thought about it. *(He ponders the question. Three or four colors of light flicker on and off. The music continues. The light, returned to pure bright white, is now however dimmer.)* I don't know exactly.

Carla: God made a firmament in the midst of the waters.

Frank: I want to see, dammit!

James: Yes. To see what you've been missing.

Carla: *(Shading her eyes, seeing a little more.)* Oh, there's a tree. A maple, look at the leaves. There's an evergreen. What kind though? *(Pause.)* God named the animals and plants. I want to know the names of everything!

Pause. The music continues but now it turns darker. Frank inexplicably speaks in a low, severe tone of voice.

Frank: Who told you that you were naked?

Carla: What, Frank?

Frank: *(Possessed by the voice.)* Who told you that you were naked? Have you eaten of the tree of which I commanded you not to eat?

Carla: You're sounding like the Bible. Why?

Frank: *(Back to his own voice.)* I don't know! The words just came out of my mouth!

Carla: James, what's going on?

Frank: *(Possessed again by the severe voice.)* What is it that you have done? Hath the serpent beguiled you? You have eaten of the tree of which I commanded you not to eat. Cursed is this ground, because of this.

Carla: I'm afraid, James. The forest isn't supposed to be like this, is it?

James: It's not the forest, Carla. It's you.

The music continues to play. Frank is himself again. He fears that this possession will occur once more. He struggles to fight it off. He jumps up and down like an upset baby.

Frank: No, no! It wasn't me.

The music brightens a bit. A golden, more mellow hue fades up and replaces the white light. The music slowly starts to build towards a climax.

Carla: *(Calmer.)* The music is vibrating. It's soothing my heart.

Frank *becomes absorbed in examining his own body. He touches it, he pinches himself. During the following dialogue he tries to figure out if he is real or if he is dreaming. He is still spooked by having been possessed by the severe voice.*

James: Carla, the ground is soft. Grass, ferns.

Carla: I don't know. This place is strange.

James: It won't be. Just wait.

Carla: I've been waiting for too long. Nothing ever seems to happen.

James: *(Gesturing to her, to come with him.)* Come on.

Carla: Maybe we should just stay right here.

The music begins its approach to its final climax.

Where's the horizon? I don't see one.

James: *(Almost to himself.)* What better place to make love than in nature.

Carla: Hey, wait a minute. Did you say, "make love"?

James: We could you know... *(He nods his head in the direction of the wings.)* move off just a little.

Carla: I told you the way I am now.

James: I had hoped we could come to some kind of understanding.

Carla: James, I do love you. It's just that I can't.

Pause. The music achieves its final climax. Now a coda-like passage begins.

James: Don't lose touch.

Carla: Are you going somewhere?!

James: You'll wait.

Carla: *(Torn.)* But I can't wait. Please. You're not going to go are you?

James: *(Looking around, musing.)* All around, space multiplies itself.

Suddenly Frank is possessed once more, this time he lets out an infant's cry.

Frank: What! Whaaaht!

Carla: A baby.

James: You've always wanted a child.

Frank *returns to himself. He is at great pains to cope with his most recent outburst. Pause.*

James: Love me. Can you?

Carla: God is love.

Pause. The music continues. Frank *begins to be able to see a little.*

Frank: *(To himself.)* Is this spring or fall or what? *(The music that plays is not his kind of music.)* And what's this music?

Carla: James, you're what I've always hoped for.

James: I've been trying to be with you.

Frank: *(Still not seeing properly.)* You'll be with her over my dead body.

Carla: This is kind of amazing. But... *(The music skids to a halt.)* is this really love? Or am I just horny? *(The music starts again, but it will never again be the same. Pause.)* You're a good man. There's something called sin. Our definitions of love are different. *(Giving up on* James.*)* This can't last. *(The music stops once and for all.* Frank *can see again. He is uncharacteristically silent—he is hearing what he would like to hear.)* My feelings are being jerked around.*(Pause.)* All this is too much like a fairy tale.*(Pause.)* I believe in God, and in Jesus, the son of God—not fairy tales. If we can't share our love for Christ and the Father then there's no basis for this relationship. *(Pause.)* I should never have gotten involved with someone who isn't in my church.

James: Most of the people that belong to your church are married.

Carla: You may be right about a lot of things but you're not right for me.

Frank: Carla, this is what I've been trying to tell you all along.

Carla: *(To* Frank.) You're no help. *(To* James.) I'm afraid. Our friendship is more important to me than it is to you. That's dangerous. I may be weak. But I have some strength. You'd better go now.

Frank: Ha, ha! Don't call us, we'll call you!

James *looks at* Frank *with a look to kill.*

James: *(Pause.)* Carla, call me if you need me.

She looks at the phone number that James *gave her beforehand.* James *walks off.*

Carla: I like him. He's nice.

Frank: Aren't they all.

Carla: If you want, I'll take a knife with me. For protection. When I go out to the forest to see him.

Frank: You just said goodbye to him.

Carla: Don't you want me to be happy?

Frank: I'll tell you: James is old enough to have a past. A criminal one.

Carla: I could forgive him if that were the case.

Frank *snatches away the piece of paper that she has been holding.*

Frank: You see this piece of paper? *(He tears it up, and eats the pieces.)* There.

Carla: Doesn't matter. I've memorized it.

Frank: Great. *(Pause.)* One of these days you might want to do something. About what's wrong with you. I can't watch out for you much longer.

Carla: I can't wash your clothes, cook your meals for much longer, either. I'm moving out.

Frank: To go where?

Carla: I've got friends. Church friends.

Frank: Sure. Hey, I have an idea. I could lend you some money to get you on your feet. A little cash from my stash of a hundred and fifty thousand. *(He pulls the check out of his shorts pocket. He displays it in front of her and glares at her. He struts around some. He tears the check up and eats it.)* So much for that. The fraud.

Carla: You're no good for me. For my spiritual well-being, I mean.

Frank: Spiritual well-being? Look. You just want to go somewhere and get laid. *(He struts around in the sand some more. Then:)* All this from a girl who says no to premarital sex. You've been oh so flexible in the past, haven't you?

Carla: You must really hate me. *(She turns away, tries to control her emotions.)* I'll call him.

Frank: He doesn't have a phone. There's no phones in the forest. Why beat yourself up over him?

Carla: I'm going to call. *(Pause.)* Maybe the money he gave you was for real.

Frank: The problem is that he doesn't exist.

Carla: Your problem is that you criticize too much. You're running out of criticisms. So what's left? Being negative. In general. About everything. Watch out. Your mind is getting fished out just like *(She looks out to the water.)* the Atlantic Ocean.

Frank: I need to exercise. Somebody around here has to stay fit. In body and in mind. You know, once you get a real job, you'll get tired the way other people get tired. You'll start watching television. It'll do you good. You'll start getting with it again. *(He does a few warm up exercises.)* I ought to make you call James. To get you out of my hair.

Carla: You said James doesn't exist.

Frank: He doesn't. *(He runs off to go jogging along the beach.)*

Carla: There's got to be some purpose to it. God, why are things so complicated? *(She gets down on the sand to pray. She leans against the beach chair. She holds back from praying at first.)* I do have to get out of here. It doesn't have to be the forest I go to. *(Pause.)* Arizona. That's where I'll go. They have Mexican style churches out there. *(Pause.)* Somebody moved out to Phoenix from here once. Who was it? Hmm. Adobe. Painted clay.

Frank *jogs back in for a moment.*

Frank: You're talking about Arizona again?

Carla: What's it to you?

Frank: First you got to get west of Albany, New York. You've never been past there. *(He jogs out.)*

Carla: Today has lasted forever. Did James say to dream of the brook and he would bring the forest, or was it the other way around? I liked the way he spoke. Most guys—they'd never speak to you about brooks and nature. And birds and trees. *(Pause.)* He seemed to be in a rush to have sex, though. Why does it have to be such a problem? Once you're married you can have it three times a day if you want to. *(Pause. She prays.)* Dear Lord, I know Jesus had to suffer. But me? It's not like I'm going against the established rule of the Roman Emperor or the Jews. *(Pause.)* I shouldn't have gotten married before. To Frank's friend. People are turned off when they hear you got divorced.

If the right guy doesn't come along soon, I'm afraid I'll find the first... No, I won't do that. Please, give me the strength to resist temptation, Lord. *(Pause. She prays and cries softly.)* How can you think about sin when you're lonely and he's lonely too? *(She stops crying. Pause. She continues to pray.)* Lord, You give me the strength but I waste it. I try to focus on what You say. You say we're all God's children—and many times I feel like a child and I want to cry, I feel like a failure and I want to die. Sometimes I get so sexually attracted to a guy... *(Pause.)* I can't say anymore, God. I'm embarrassed to talk to even You anymore.

She sluggishly gets up from her prayers and slides into her beach chair. She turns her head to one side. She closes her eyes. A brief pause. James *enters. He takes off his clothes and has a bathing suit on. He sits down in the other beach chair. Carla has dozed off in the sun.* James *suns himself in his chair. After a minute, he gently touches Carla's arm, to wake her up.*

James: Carla, you've fallen asleep.

Carla: *(Groggy.)* What?

James: Wake up. You don't want to get sunburned.

Carla: *(Waking.)* You're back. *(Sweetly.)* Oh, James.

James: Now that I've got my bathing suit on I don't feel like swimming.

Carla: I'm ready. *(She points to the ocean.)*

James: For the forest.

Carla: Yes. Look at it. Leaves, vines, moss. I'll be the brook.

James: We should take a blanket.

Carla: We'll go just as we are. I'll be the brook and the forest will be very happy. I'll make sure of that.

Pause. Carla *and* James *freeze. We hear the sound of ocean waves. A few moments later as* Frank *enters slowly there is music.* Frank *drags a fisherman's net across the sand behind him. In the net is a wooden cross, the size of a man. The net and the cross are wet and glistening, having just come out of the sea. After* Frank *crosses the stage the music ends. Blackout. The play ends.*

Behave, My Sorrow

a solo play
for an actor and his puppet

The words, "Behave, My Sorrow" are from the first line, in English, of a poem by Charles Baudelaire entitled *Recueillement* ("Meditation"). Part of this poem is paraphrased at the end of the play.

A powerful formal influence upon this play were the ritual plays I saw in performance at Japan House in New York in November of 1997. They were presented by the Awaji Puppet Theater, from Awaji Island, Japan.

There will always be the question at the end of this piece whether or not Rachel broke off contact with Bruno because of his religious background. This play is an attempt at catharsis for Bruno; at the end we see it is a purification ritual for him. The older the actor playing Bruno, perhaps the more poignant the proceedings.

The various voices that Bruno must use are bolded merely for clarity. This play is an etude, a theatrical exercise for a solo actor, as well as being a "performance art" piece.

The play was presented in a public reading by Walter Teres at Hart House, in Toronto on September 19, 1998. It is dedicated to him.

The Characters

Bruno   Male, of short height, late 20s to
early 50s.

Place: Starts as a neutral space.

Time: The present.

Behave, My Sorrow

The Scene

A spotlight comes up for Bruno. Bruno *enters talking. He has a sock puppet on one hand and a pail in his other hand. The pail is filled with water; also in the pail is a drinking cup. He sets the pail down.*

The puppet, who starts out as Buddy, *is also used for the character of the* Woman—*in her various accents and voice pitches, for example, high voice, Southern accent, etc.*

Buddy: *(That is, the puppet, to* Bruno.) Hey, stone face, you got rocks in your head or something?

Bruno: *(To his sock puppet.)* What?

Buddy: You got rocks in your head, you crazy or something?

Bruno: I feel like I'm going crazy.

Buddy: Then you got rocks in your head. (Buddy *snaps his head quickly back and forth. It is accompanied by the sound of rocks being shaken in a canister.)* Still thinking of her, Bruno? *(Pause. Of course* Bruno *is. He does not reply, though. Pause.)* I want to become a computer engineer.

Bruno: Oh, yeah—

Buddy: I want to make lots of money. And I don't want to be tied to anyone.

Bruno: Buddy, you don't like me?

Buddy: You're okay. Bruno. I could become a doctor. Or lawyer.

Bruno: You could—

Buddy: And make lots of money.

Bruno: Yep.

Buddy: But is that all there is to life?, I ask myself. No, of course not. That's why I'll be like Andrew Carnegie. After I've made my pile, I'll go the non-materialistic route. *(Pause.)* I'm gonna bite you. (Bruno *ignores him.)*

Bruno: You'll be a patron of the arts.

Buddy: Yes, I will learn to appreciate the Greeks. Hey, what's that pail doing there anyway? *(He refers to the pail down at Bruno's feet.)*

Bruno: Don't worry about it, Buddy.

Buddy: Me? Okay. *(Pause.)* I'm going to make my money then throw it all away.
    (Sings:) I'm going to make my money, throw it all away.

Bruno: That would be very nice of you.

Buddy: Crazy, if you ask me. Still, you can't take it with you, can you? *(Pause.)* That's why I've got another, better plan.

Buddy *whispers his plan in Bruno's ear.*

Bruno: You're going to start your own religion—

Buddy: Not a bad idea, huh?

Bruno: What do you know about religion?

Buddy: All that needs to be known. You have to be able to talk. A lot. That I can do. The next thing is to get followers.

Bruno: Is it that easy to get people to follow you?

Buddy: Sure. You have to give 'em the business.

Bruno: The business?

Buddy: I'll show you. Here's a common one: *(Pause.)* Woman, you must become a Catholic.

The Woman *is also Bruno's sock puppet; it is most advantageous when all voices are strongly distinguishable from one another in pitch and accent.*

Woman: Catholic? What's that?

Buddy: The only way to live.

Woman: Really?

Buddy: You're going to Hell if you don't believe.

Woman: Really?

Buddy: Can you afford to be wrong?

Woman: Things aren't too horrible now.

Buddy: They'll get worse. You'd better convert.

Woman: What if I don't?

Buddy: We are conquerors. We will kill you if you don't.

Woman: I will seek eternal happiness with your religion. I want to live. I want to live!

Buddy: We will love you. (Buddy *turns to* Bruno.) There, that's how it's done.

Bruno: I'm impressed.

Buddy: It works with all the religions. Look— *(To another woman.)* Woman, you must become part of the nation of Islam.

Woman: What's that?

Buddy: The only way to live.

Woman: Really?

Buddy: You're going to Hell if you don't believe.

Woman: Will I be treated with respect?

Buddy: If you honor and obey God and your husband.

Woman: I have a little freedom now. What are you exactly offering me?

Buddy: It's what *God* offers you.

Woman: So there's only one God?

Buddy: Get rid of all the rest.

Woman: Is one enough?

Buddy: More than enough, and He has caused a Holy Book to be written.

Woman: You mean God can write?

Buddy: Yes, basically.

Woman: I can't read.

Buddy: You'll have to take my word for it. I will kill you if you don't.

Woman: I believe. I believe!

Buddy: We will love you. (Buddy *turns to* Bruno.) It works just like that.

Bruno: You use fear to your maximum advantage.

Buddy: Don't be talking like a sophomore in college!

Bruno: So having your own religion is going to make you happy.

Buddy: Life never gets boring when you're the center of attention.

Bruno: Try to convert someone to Judaism.

Buddy: You think you can slip me up with that one, huh?

Bruno: They don't look for converts.

Buddy: Yeah, sure, I've heard that one before. They're not going to turn their noses up at a little more money in their coffers.

Buddy *nods this way and that way, he wails as if he is standing at the Wailing Wall in Jerusalem. He stops.*

Buddy: *(To another woman.)* Woman, I know you like ritual. Everybody likes ritual. The repetitions ease the mind. The decision-making process is disabled, all is given over to the rhythm of the moment.

Woman: I like ritual.

Buddy: I want to tell you about a religion.

Woman: I'm already a believer.

Buddy: Not in Judaism. *(Pause.)* You have a daughter?

Woman: Yes, why do you ask?

Buddy: Are you worried about her?

Woman: How did you know?

Buddy: It's the ways of the world.

Woman: You're a very knowing and experienced person.

Buddy: I'm acquainted with a friendly and secure man. Your daughter could marry him. The catch is, she must convert to his religion. He's a Jew. His God won't let him marry just anybody.

Woman: I understand. But my daughter and I will go to Hell if we break our present faith in our own God.

Buddy: You like ritual, right? Pay attention to me. I am a rabbi, your teacher. Avoid contact with other human eyes. Even the eyes of pets. Now. I have this scripture here. You only chant with me. We are to take these words of God, chanting lineo-mix in the circular, cyclo-mix in the linear. During this sacred process you will feel new waves smashing over old waves. Your old faith will be battered, bathed, and rubbed out. I chant lineo-mixture-wise: *(In a thick "Hebrew" accent:) Eb fa ke vim gridge.* Then cyclo-mix in the linear: *Gridge fa ke vim eb.*

Woman: Is that Hebrew?

Buddy: It's a very sacred language, lady.

Woman: Okay, I'll repeat it.
  Eb fa ke vim gridge.
  Gridge fa ke vim eb.

Buddy: Very good! Now you're a Jew. Wait for me outside. Later we'll go find your daughter and convert her too.

Woman: I'll make sure my daughter will marry your Jewish man. Weeuu! I'll be glad to get her off my mind.

Buddy: Oh, lady, I forgot to tell you. You are *loved.*

Bruno: Okay, that's enough, Buddy.

Buddy: Let there be light.

Bruno: No, no. Not until I say so. Don't get ahead of me. The music has to come up first. Let me focus, okay? I need to. Focus on the things that got me into this in the first place. (*He momentarily puts his free hand to his forehead to try to calm himself.*)

Buddy: You gave it away by mentioning the Jewish subject matter just at the end.

Bruno: I'm focusing. Goodbye. (*He sets down the sock puppet. He momentarily puts his free hand again to his forehead. He gains some poise.*) Okay, I'm ready. (*He commands.*) Start sonic perimeter. (*Some music is turned on. Pause.*) Fine. (*He commands again.*) Now, raise the fear-reflectors. (*We hear the electronic sound of a set of "fear reflectors" come out of their bays and lock into the raised position.* Bruno *addresses the audience:*) If there's any fear it will be bounced out back into deep space, into nothingness. (*He commands once more.*) Okay, let it rip—

A surge of wonderful music and sound occurs just as the lights fade up on a human figure clad in a space suit, suspended from a rope. The figure looks over the stage floor and across to the audience. *In back, or to the side of the dummy of the astronaut, we see the line coming from the pulley that helps hold it up. The line is tied to a fixture attached to the floor.*

Bruno *jumps up and down with glee at the sight of the floating effigy. He runs around below the figure, looks, cheers its presence. Then the music fades, but is still heard faintly.*

Bruno: I'm up there, *(He points up to the figure.)* looking down. Me, Bruno Castini. The world's cracks don't show up in space, no religions, no divisions. Say a prayer for life the beautiful.

(Pause.) Come join me, Rachel, in the hammock of sweet space, we'll rest. Then we'll go walking. We'll wear suits sewn into existence by the string section of the Paris Symphony Orchestra, conducted by André Kostelantez.

But you can only love a Jewish man you say, and I'm not Jewish. I know you told me that early when me met. I had hoped love would conquer all.

Come down, Rachel.

He goes and unties the rope that is tied to the floor. He lowers the figure part way and ties the rope securely. He talks to the figure. Though the figure can represent Bruno, at this moment it represents Rachel.

Bruno: Rachel, I am driven to see this end. *(Pause.)*
We meet your father. He's from that city he wants to move to after he divorces your mom. He likes to argue. He's always right. I've never met him before. But he's down on the launch pad. His theme is that you are to only marry a Jewish man. He shakes my hand, or does he? He's the one you say, that's always been there for you. You're not going to do anything to make him unhappy.

You've been making the rounds of the launch pads, yes. Trying to find a Jewish astronaut. Why won't you listen to me? You know they don't exist, ...that you're looking for something that's an impossibility.

I'm destroyed. And your time is wasted. *I've* got a rocket. Is there anything wrong with me? Besides not being from one of the—what is it—thirteen tribes? Step away from this earth. See it as a blue-green, round, swan. *(Pause.)*

Let your heart *feel,* Rachel. Rise, don't let your religion be so cruel. *(Pause.)*

A truck skirts the launch pad, a fuel truck, your father's driving it. Under no circumstances, says he, can your husband be a convert. He must be *born* a Jew. Oh, but look at your father now. He radios the Sun-God, named Ra. He'd never admit that to you. He wants order, that much I understand. We all want calm.

Doesn't it matter that we have so many other things in common? Well, you don't want me. You're ready for someone else. Maybe you're ready for nobody.

He goes over to the rope, unties it, and raises the effigy to its initial position.

Bruno: I'm in space, it's the only space for me now. The only one far better alternative would be for me to rest my head upon your breast. *(Pause. He goes and picks up the sock puppet.)* Buddy, I'm in bad shape.

Buddy: You're down and out, man. *Really* down and out. You got two choices. You either get religion or you kill yourself.

Bruno: Which religion do you want me to get?

Buddy: Mine, of course.

Bruno: Which is?

Buddy: First you have to stop thinking about Rachel. You think she's being too picky, and it's stupid because what she wants, she'll never get. You have to walk away, my friend. Forget about her. Thus I teach the religion of walking away and forgetting.

Bruno: Sounds more like a *philosophy* than a religion.

Buddy: Welcome to the new millennium, my friend.

Bruno: Yes, maybe metaphysical belief is best for our times.

Buddy: You bet it is. Philosophy even worked liked religion in the twentieth century. Where have you been? Listen: *(To a woman.)* Woman, you must become a Communist.

Woman: What's that?

Buddy: The only way to live.

Woman: Really?

Buddy: You'll be exploited for the rest of your life if you don't become a Communist.

Woman: But will I be free?

Buddy: Yes, there will be no poverty.

Woman: But will I be compelled to march in parades?

Buddy: That's a small price to pay for future generations in the perfect society.

Woman: Who said anything about future generations?

Buddy: If we can't manage to get things perfect now, there's always the future.

Woman: What about now?

Buddy: You're being selfish. If you don't consider others and pull together with us all we will liquidate you.

Woman: Liquidate?

Buddy: We will kill you if you don't become a Communist. *(In a hysterical voice.)* Kill! Kill!

Woman: I will become one.

Buddy: Become one with us all. We will *like* you very much.

Bruno: Well, Buddy, thanks for cheering me up.

Buddy: You should be cheerful. You've got years ahead of you. How are you going to use those years?

Bruno: Are you pressuring me?

Buddy: Is life meaningless unless you have love?

Bruno: Yes, you are pressuring me. I'm already ready to burst, that's why I need to get above the planet and see it from that perspective.

Buddy: You don't want to get too removed from it all.

Bruno: Yeah, what do you know—

Buddy: *(To the audience:)* Look at the state he's in.
And this my friends is what unrequited love
    can do
    to you.

Bruno: Don't be cruel.

Buddy: Act like this and you're not going to get ahead in the world.

Bruno: This world. Where Jewish astronauts do not exist.

Buddy: Love. Forget her. Come join me and the other computer engineers. We'll make lots of money.

Bruno: You're a little devil.

Buddy: I'm your buddy.

Bruno: Take this, buddy. (*He goes over to the pail and bends at his knees. He plunges* Buddy *into the water.*)

Buddy: What?

Bruno: We're not as powerful as we think.

Buddy: Don't get mad. Get rich.

Bruno: I'm going to wash you out my life.

Buddy: You're picking on the wrong guy. What have I ever done to you? Drown your sorrows, but don't drown me! I'm your clown, your jester. I'm what keeps the king going on a bad day.

Bruno: Oh, shut up. And die!

Buddy: What are you doing this for?

Bruno: I'm crazy. You know it. You've said it.

Buddy: Blub-blub. Blub-blub. (Bruno *then takes the wet sock off his hand and wrings it out into the pail. He throws the sock down on the ground.*

Bruno: (*To the audience:*)
Behave, my sorrow—let's have no more scenes.

(As if to a child:)
Quiet down, quiet down. You've got Night, now,
—It's fallen; see how it overtakes the town,
Bringing peace to some, to others pain...

You called for Night, now, give me your hand,
I'll lead you far from the vile multitude of mortals,
They who abide under the whip of Pleasure,
That merciless executioner.

Planetarium music fades in. The lights come up on the effigy of the astronaut. Bruno *takes the hand of the effigy and kisses it softly. He then goes over to the pail, picks it up, and the wet sock also. He goes over to the effigy, dunks the sock into the pail. He takes the wet puppet out of the water and wrings the water from it slowly, drizzling and sprinkling water along the length of the effigy, and even some water upon himself.*

Nature, whose waters fall on the good and wrong alike.
Pronounce me and you *(He gestures to the effigy.)* cleansed.

The music plays. The lights fade to black and the play ends.

Live Free or Die

an outdoor play

Though this play is written for outdoor performance it may be played indoors.

Besides being indebted to Japanese form and subject matter in *Live Free Or Die* I am also influenced by situations, action and characters of Medieval English theatricals—skits, pageants, mummers' plays, etc.

There remains the nagging fact that nearly two million Americans are incarcerated, about half of them on drug convictions. The majority of citizens do not seem to care that such people are simply being warehoused; local economies are boosted by the building of more prisons. I am looking to achieve a richness here that telling the "prison story" in a linear, journalistic fashion would not make possible.

This play is dedicated to Jeanne Stebnisky.

The Characters

Flags Man	Male, 40s or 50s. Though Canadian, he may have a non-North American accent (not thick). This actor is also a member of the Chorus.
Actress/Amanda	Female, late 20s to mid 30s. For the role of Amanda she wears a wig of long, full hair.
William	Male. Early thirties.
Herald	Female or male. Also a member of the Chorus.
Professor/ Chorus Leader	Female or male. When no immediate conflict in roles exists s/he is a member of the Chorus.
Trudi	Female. Late 20s to early 30s.
Hernando/ Tea Assistant	Male. Under the age of 45.
Tea Master	Female, 30s to 70s. During the first three-fourths of the play she is a Chorus member. (She is absent from the Chorus beginning with the line, *"When man is contrite..."*)

Place: Various places not far from Lake Ontario, in both Canada and New York state.

Time: August, the late 1990's.

Live Free or Die

The Prelude to the Play

The Scene

In a park in Toronto. A colorful banner hangs between two trees—or two poles if there are no trees in the outdoor playing area. We may notice that a yard-long twisted stick lies on the ground. (The stick is to remain in the playing area until William *picks it up later.) Next to a pushcart that is jammed with small flags from around the world stands the* Flags Man. *He is slightly hunched, as if standing under a low roof. The* Actress *enters and nearly walks by the* Flags Man *but he stops her.*

Flags Man: Where y' going?

Actress: Inside.

Flags Man: What? You're not going to do your play?

Actress: It's started to rain.

Flags Man: Just a drop here and there. It won't last.

Actress: Not too many people showed up.

Flags Man: A few clouds in the sky. Big deal. In High Park they'd put on the play.

Actress: *I* didn't call it off. The director did.

Flags Man: Shakespeare and rain go together like toast and jam. The group that does it in the other park knows that.

Actress: We're a smaller operation.

Flags Man: Then you should have your heart in it.

Actress: It is. Is your heart in what you're doing? You're *selling* your flags.

Flags Man: Toronto's not cheap.

Actress: We're doing this for free.

Flags Man: You don't have to be smug about it.

Actress: Look, this isn't High Park. You should probably go back to the Danforth.

Flags Man: A pity about those who came to see a play. *(He wants to see one.)*

Actress: Sorry. They can come back tomorrow.

Flags Man: Then it might really rain. The director should reconsider.

Actress: She's gone home.

He holds his hand out into the air.

Flags Man: See, it's stopped. 'Must take you actors a while to come all the way out here.

Actress: Yeah—

Flags Man: You should practice as long as you're here.

Actress: Half the cast has already left.

Flags Man: Don't you have another play? A smaller one? I bet your cast is all warmed up.

Actress: They were, actually.

Flags Man: There's still a some of you—

Actress: Yeah, they're my friends.

Flags Man: The diehards.

Actress: Yep.

Flags Man: The serious ones. I can tell. Come on, you must have another play you're working on—

Actress: *(Hesitating.)* It's not a Shakespeare play.

Flags Man: Ah, who cares? You can see that anytime in the summer, rain or shine, in good old High Park. Hey, there are still a few people here. They'd love to see a play.

Actress: They might not go for it.

Flags Man: Has it got sex in it?

Actress: There are suggestions.

Flags Man: Good, good. *(Long pause. In a reverie.)* How I like a drama. I see enough of the plain truth from my pushcart.

Actress: I don't know if we can do the play. One of the guys that's in it took off.

Flags Man: It's a Canadian play. You'll find some way to make it work.

Actress: Actually it's not a Canadian play. It's from the U.S.

Flags Man: Tennessee Williams?

Actress: No.

Flags Man: I like him. Is he still alive?

Actress: He's always be alive. This is a new play. Brand new.

Flags Man: Is it a hit?

Actress: Not to my knowledge.

Flags Man: So why are you doing an American play?

Actress: It's not just an American story. It's... universal.

Flags Man: Well, then it's for me.

Actress: The only problem is that Harold's already gone. We need him for the chorus. Can I ask you a favor?

Flags Man: Maybe.

Actress: I'd like you to fill in for him.

Flags Man: I couldn't possibly do that.

Actress: Oh, come on. I thought you wanted us to do a play.

Flags Man: I do.

Actress: Well then, help us out. You'll only have a few lines alone. But they're very important.

Flags Man: Alone? I thought I just had to be in the chorus. All of a sudden I'm by myself, I'm feeling sick. (*Histrionically, comically.*) I can't go through with it.

Actress: That's stage fright.

Flags Man: The people—they'll be looking at me.

Actress: You'll feel better once you're in the swing of it.

Flags Man: Says who?

Actress: Generations of actors.

Flags Man: Where are they now?

Actress: Dead.

Flags Man: See, it killed them. (*The sound of thunder and rain is heard.*) Oh, it's raining again.

Actress: No. That's just the sound of the storm in our new play. Come with me.

The Actress *leads the* Flags Man, *with his cart, out of the playing area. If the play is performed indoors the lights will fade out here. This is the end of the prelude.*

The Play Proper

Sounds of thunder and rain continue. Stormy music begins. We are in a Renaissance Fair's parking lot, in a field, in New York state, not far from Lake Ontario. (An adjacent meadow figures into the action later. Still later the play travels to Canada. At all times the colorful banner that is displayed during the prelude remains.)

Trudi *and* Amanda, *in medieval dress, enter. They hold newspapers to protect their heads from the rain. They hurry across the playing area and out.* Hernando, *in medieval clothing, leads a horse across the playing area. The horse is the* Flags Man's *pushcart, cloaked in black, with a cloth horse-head sticking out of it.* Hernando *carries an umbrella to keep away the rain as he crosses the playing area. We notice that the horse has a couple of national flags sticking out of its body.* Hernando *and his horse exit the playing area. The* Chorus *enters.*

Chorus:
    By the inland sea, Ontario,
    The winds blast away at the slate shore,
    There is a clamor upon the American pastures,
    A grave downpour—
    This unloosens the concrete convict-castle
    That squats looking out towards Canada:
    Stagger Lee Prison it's called,
    Stacked catacombs with razor-fence spools atop.
    Of course, this is the haughty, towering pillory
    That punishes bad men,
    Its outside formidable, its inside, a lordly
    Fortress of dubious fairness—but look,

What a surprise! The uprooted reformatory
Is detached, it's blown out past the bay,
On its side it floats back again to land—
The same large land that Rochester, Buffalo, the
Iroquois and sixty small New York state towns love,
Despite being often squalled upon.
It appears that this penitentiary has had
Its steel locks picked by the storm,
For its incarceration doors swing carefree
After the gale is gone.
One still-breathing inmate emerges;
Squeezing out from between the twisted bars,
He wanders free from the sharp-wire barricade.

One Chorus Member:
Questioning the how and wherefore of this storm,
Upon the saltless great lake
I am told of...

Chorus:
Two grapplers wrestling in the atmosphere, their names
being Big Lonely Deep Freeze—from the Arctic, and
Heavy Hulk Sky Master, from the tropical south.

William *enters, wet. The* Chorus *continues:*

There upon the wet grass, near the battered, low
    smooth hills:
The prisoner shakes his foot free,
He's been coughed up by heaving fate,
This is the man of whom you are to hear.
He is by luck of the tempest delivered from the prison
    clear.
Now he makes his way to a meadow.

The storm sounds and stormy music die down. The Chorus
looks up to the sky momentarily and continues.

• 251

Oh, what sun. You don't see that sun in the Big House. No, the sun there is manacled, single beams, troubled, dodge metal bolts to be slightly seen.

Members of the Chorus *look at* William *and continue:*

An odd sensation for the con: to be tramping about. He has spent five long winters on the lowest human rung, enclosed in that Stagger Lee North. There's but one month left to his sentence, that doesn't matter now, he has his release.

William *exits. A* Herald, *who has been in the* Chorus, *comes forward.*

Herald: *(With a fake Elizabethan accent.)*
 Hear ye, hear ye.
 By the Lord that sheddeth his mysterious blood,
 We pray you enjoy our food and cheer
 And may ye better lords and ladies be
 Upon leaving our games;
 Feel free to return to us,
 In your reveries.

The Herald *steps back to join the* Chorus *again.* Trudi *enters. She is in a suit of armor. She wears a burgonet—a visored helmet. She comes in with a large flat ax mounted atop a pole; She "patrols" the parking lot.*

Chorus Leader: What's this? A medieval guard patrolling a modern field?

Chorus:
 Love. Do not despair.
 The dark cloud has passed.
 He has emerged from his confinement
 To find his Lady at last.

William *enters again.*

William:
They made me a captive in body
But never in mind.
How I've suffered for their fears,
Their highhandedness.
Marijuana. I sold it.
We joked and called it tea.
It once provided refuge from the uncaring world,
Till that world started caring for me—dearly.
In short, they apprehended me.
I and my cocaine brothers, how we jam the prison log,
Each sorted to cages like leper-dogs.

Trudi *has not seen or heard* William *until now. She speaks in the low tones of man, with a faux Elizabethan accent as well:*

Trudi:
Sirrah, thou know'st how Orleans is besieged
And how the English have the suburbs won.

William: What? *(Pause. He continues walking.)*

Trudi: Stand ho! Friend or foe? You shall not survive your treachery.

William: I'm a friend. A friend. Where am I?

Trudi: Unfold yourself.

William: Have I gone back in time?

Trudi: Be you from France? Be you from Troy?

William: *(To himself.)* Or have things changed so much while I've been away? Maybe the televisions just play tapes to us.

Trudi:
> Thou art a knave. Dangerous, sly,
> With no noble honors
> To support your similitude.

William: You're wrong. I'm not a danger to anybody. *(Pause.)* Why are you dressed like that?

Trudi: Better me to ask why thou appearest in thine attire.

William: It's been a bad storm.

Trudi: Our patch of Atlas's globe is yet a muddy mire. *(Pause.)* Where's your car, yeoman?

William: I don't have a car.

Trudi: Why are you then in King Arthur's parking lot?

William: I hitch-hiked. They let me off near here. *(Pause.)* Your voice—don't I know you?

Trudi: *(Speaking in her feminine voice.)* 'Zounds, the troubles are just beginning. You would fain compromise a maid?

William: I thought you were a woman.

Trudi: *(Shooing him away.)* Disperse, disperse. The crowds of our fair have ridden off because of the rain.

William: It's not you, Trudi. Is it?

Trudi: *(She lifts up her helmet visor and ends her medieval impersonation.)* William?

William: It is you. *(Pause. They reach and touch one another briefly.)*

Trudi: Don't you have one more month to go of your sentence?

William: The prison got washed out into the lake. Instead of going down we washed back in.

Trudi: Oh, William. *(His presence "sinks" in. She embraces him.)* It's great to see you.

William: And you, too.

Trudi: Hang on for a minute. *(She leaves.)*

William:
> Am I really free? Free!?
> A stabbing daylight greets me,
> Who's behind the knife?
> Who wants what from me?
> Is this taste some bait
> To get me to inform?
> But I don't talk,
> I tell on no one.
> I never did, not even the first year.
>
> Now a breeze unfazed by walls smoothes my face.
> How otherworldly it feels,
> Like the first feel of rubber—a black bicycle tube—
> When I was a boy.
> Oh, injuries, wounds of isolation.
> They cannot be healed by a strange and novel, but
>   welcome, wind.
> The seclusion has brought with it a horrible din.
> It cackles my ears up with sore memories.
> Ah, Time rots if you don't garden it.
> I did. I did.
> Though for Time to come ripe you need to go outside.

I'm sure Amanda works here too. She said she had a new job.

Hernando *enters.*

Hernando: Hmpf! *(He looks* William *up and down.)* You're the man from the "escape-proof" Stagger Lee Prison.

William: There was a storm.

Hernando: Yeah, sure, sure. How did you do it?

William: I didn't do anything.

Hernando: That's what they all say. You got one month to go. Boy, you're stupid to bust out.

William: I told you—

Hernando: You're past thirty now. You should know better.

William: *(Recognizing him.)* The county lockup. When I was first arrested. The Puerto Rican, right?

Hernando: No way, man. I've never been in the slammer.

William: Yeah, before I was sentenced to Stagger Lee. You were such a show-off. And you almost killed me.

Hernando: All us Latinos look the same to you. And you think we're jailbirds, too. Actually, I'm from Canada. Well, I'm a *new* Canadian— I was born in Chile. I play the Turk or the Moorish prince here at the fair. Sometimes they got me playing Sir Dennis. I joust with the white knight, the English guy. Not bad, eh?—for a kid from Quebrada de Alvarado, Aconcagua.

I tell you, the chicks here are amazing. Their boobs are lifted up and half exposed. Santa Maria!, I love these Renaissance fairs.

Chorus: (Women Only.)
   Tra-la-la-la-la, la-la
   Renaissance fair.

Hernando: Ah, It's nice to work both sides of the border. This your first time seeing us?

William: (*Sarcastically.*) King Arthur's a friend of mine. I told him he'd do much better with a circular table for his pals.

Hernando: (*Deadpan.*) You're joshing me.

William: Well, I did take a course in Early English Lit. (*A horse whinnies.* Hernando *starts to exit.*) Where are you going?

Hernando *stops and looks* William *up and down.*

Hernando: I got business, man. (*He leaves.*)

William: Everybody seems so anxious to leave me alone.

Pause. William *looks out into the distance. Hubbub. The* Chorus *enters carrying a dead person—actually a mass of sticks (some twisted, all with bark still attached)—atop a stretcher.*

Chorus: (*Chanting slowly, softly.*)
   Dry. Dry. Bone dry.
   Rain gone. Fruit gone.
   How short the time of bloom,
   How long
   The time for things to go wrong.

The Chorus *repeats their chant softly, still marching. They march out of the playing area; from "off stage:*

Chorus: (Women Only.)
>Tra-la-la-la-la, la-la,
>Renaissance fair.
>Gone are the withered rotting reeds of autumn,
>Gone are the winter snows, the frozen waterfalls.

Hernando *re-enters.*

Hernando: *(To* William.) Hey, come on. If you hurry we can still catch Trudi. We'll sneak up and watch her as she changes her clothes. (William *ignores him.* Hernando *exits.* William *peers into the distance.)*

William: Alone. *(Pause.)* At least I did something with the time.

A Professor *enters in cap and gown. S/he holds a diploma. S/he shakes it at* William *while speaking.*

Professor:
>The anger of Achilles, the devastation it brings,
>The piling up of bodies in Hades,
>Are these pivotal traumas necessary today?
>In the past, Homer centralized.
>But it is the limbs,
>The body, ...the Body, Desire—
>Lacan, Derrida. Foucault.
>The French. Desire. The Body.
>Who needs the Greeks, the Will?
>There is no center except the self,
>And the self is actually mental sprawl.
>There are suburbs, yes. A Downtown? No.
>I am speaking metaphorically,
>However I'm being analytical.

William: I don't agree with you.

Professor: You don't have to. But you must concur with me.

William: I don't concur, professor.

Professor: Then you must concede.

William: I don't concede.

Professor: Thank you for agreeing.

William: I'm not. Can't we compromise?

Professor: I'm sorry but you are to receive a failing grade. *(Pause.)* Through the dark jungle, we have found and deconstructed a clearing where there are morsels to hold, but what claim do me have to them? Perhaps they are the bits of another sex. Or an exploited sexual preference.

William: *(Holding his head in pain.)* I can't take it.

Professor: Of course you can. You're just uncomfortable with your own oppression.

William: Your words. I don't understand them.

Professor: I'm awarding you below an "F". You get an "E".

William: Isn't "G" below an "F"?

Professor: Oh, but you're forgetting about inversions.

William: I'm dropping your course.

Professor: It's too late, too late.

William: I've decided to take "Pre-Modern Philosophy" instead.

Professor: You're incarcerated. This means you cannot change your schedule. Normal people possibly drop and add. But you're an *outsider*. I also teach a course in Camus and Sartre.

William: I've contacted the administration at Empire State College.

Professor: *(Disdainfully.)* Distance Learning!

William: They say I can register for another class, but you're still my advisor.

Professor: Ha, ha! I've got you!

The Professor *of philosophy walks off, nose proudly in the air. Nearby* Trudi *and* Amanda *enter, both in modern dress, carrying parts of newspapers.*

Amanda: "Senior Retail Sales Manager. Sales Team Leaders and Professional Interviewers."

Trudi: "Blue Jean Jobs, Assembly."

Amanda: "Teach English in Japan."

William: *(Speaking across to them.)* I hitched a ride out here. Somebody picked me up from New Hampshire. You know what the plates on their cars say, "Live Free Or Die."

The women do not hear William. *They sit down on the ground and spread the newspaper out and continue to read.*

Trudi: "Bookstore. Full and part time. Excellent book knowledge and retail experience required." There's a job for William once he gets out.

Amanda: "Farm Supervisor. Vegetables, livestock, farm by the lake. Send resume." *(She reads another page of the paper.)* "If today is your birthday" ... it isn't. "You are capable of handling responsibility. When the pressure's on, you're up to it. Aquarius and Leo persons play amazing roles in your life. They're likely to have these letters as initials: I, R, W.

Trudi: Used to be people spent their Sundays going to church. Now they browse the want-ads instead.

Amanda: *(Still reading.)* "Sagittarian makes a surprise announcement."

Trudi: Hey, they've got jobs at the Renaissance Fair. Working outside—you can't beat that for the summer. At least the next time we're looking for new jobs we'll be able to spread out the paper in some field or something.

Amanda: Who do I know that's Sagittarian?

Trudi: "Frontier Communications." 'Sounds interesting. "Collect payments on bad debts." That's *very* uninteresting.

Amanda: If you were a computer geek you'd have it made.

Trudi: How about you, if you were one—

Amanda: I'd have it made, too. I didn't mean to insult you.

Trudi: Let's work both at the Renaissance Fair. We'll share the driving.

Amanda: Maybe can stay over night there sometimes. *(Pause.)* We're only putting off the inevitable. An office job. The straight and narrow. You get more out of circles than dead-end lines.

Trudi: Let's enjoy this while we can.

The women continue to read the paper, but in silence.
Hernando *enters, sword in hand. He approaches* William.

Hernando: *(To* William.) Pick up your sword.

William: What? Is there one?

Hernando: *(Fiercely.)* Somewhere. You'll find it. *(Softer.)* I'll
fight you for the maidens.

William: For them? *(He gestures to* Trudi *and* Amanda.)

Hernando: Yeah, them.

William: Wow, Amanda's here.

Hernando: We fight, winner takes both of them.

William: What if they don't want the winner?

Hernando: Yeah, they want a loser. Like you. Ha-ha!

William: I don't want to fight you.

Hernando: But you will.

William: You tried this before. In jail.

Hernando: No way, man. You're all messed up.

William: I almost died.

Hernando *shakes his head "no", treating* William *like an
uncomprehending child.*

Hernando: The knight who wins the sword fight gets to
have an orgy with the maidens. En garde. *(He raises his
sword.)* Think you're too white for me, huh? Next, you're

262 •

going to tell me the three great evils that beset the land. (William *is forced to pick up a stick—the stick that has been lying on the ground—to defend himself. The sword-and-stick fight begins. While they fight,* Hernando *continues:)* One. The spoiling of gallant youths through bad education.

Chorus: *(Off to the side.)* Testosterone. Oh, boy. Organize it, so it doesn't get ugly.

Hernando: Two. *(The fight continues.)* The degradation of good art through incompetent criticism. Three. The waste of fine tea through the careless making of it.

The sword-and-stick combat continues. Hernando *stabs* William, *who falls to the ground.*

Chorus: Too late.

Hernando: *(Full of bravura.)* I show the kingdom who is truly Champion. If there's any of you out there who think you're stronger, come forth. I say, come forth! *(He drops to his knees to aid* William.) Don't worry. It probably isn't serious. After all, this is medium security, no killers here.

(In a comic style.) I'll be your doctor, I'll un-wound what's been done. First, the pulse. *(He checks* William's *pulse.)* Oh, it's pulsing, that's a good sign.

Now, just lie there. I'll see what's happening with the Ladies in the Royal Viewing Stand. Some girl's got to be a nurse there. One look from the little darling and you'll be cured.

Trudi *comes over to them.*

Trudi: What's wrong?

Hernando: He swooned. He should have drank tea. It intimidates the enemy and instills confidence in retainers.

Trudi: What do you mean, he swooned?

Hernando: He's very tired. He needed to swoon. I know in earlier times only women did. Their dresses were too tight— all that pressure of holding in their sexual energy—too much for them. Now men swoon. But for different reasons: it's the stress of our industrial world. It bursts their buttons, if you know what I mean.

Trudi: I didn't know you had a higher education.

Hernando: *(Proudly.)* Self-taught.

William: *(Murmurs.)*
I swooned because I was stabbed.
Be grateful that you are not as me,
Forsaken, moaning before the penitentiary.
Where's Amanda?

Hernando: Ah, yes, Amanda.

William *faints and speaks no more.*

Trudi: I'm here, William, it's me.

Hernando: Trudi, admit it—I'm everything a woman wants. Before I got into this business I used to design software. Virtual reality. *Realidad virtual.* But I missed the physical sensation of the real thing. *(Macho.)* I'll give you anything you want.

Trudi: Why *give* something to me? *(Humoring him.)* Let's steal something together.

Hernando: Ooh, that's bad, very sexy. *(He looks up to the banner stretched between the two trees.)* The banner. Let's steal that. We'll cut it down.

Trudi: Good. Give me your sword.

Hernando: *You'll* cut it down?

Trudi: With pleasure.

Hernando: *(He gives her his sword.)* It'll be our secret together. But how are you going to get up there? Let me get the horse.

Trudi: Don't go back to the stables. *(In a husky voice.)* I want you here.

Hernando: Yes, baby, yes.

Trudi: I'll cut it off right now.

Sword in hand, she pretends to study the banner and how it is attached.

Hernando: Look at her. *(He cocks his head to the side and eyes her behind.)* How I look forward to the ride.

Trudi: You say something?

Hernando: I said, but there's no ladder.

Trudi: I don't need one I can reach it from right here.

She deftly places the sword blade at his crotch.

Hernando: Hey, just what are you cutting off, baby?

Trudi: A quick slice in and then off with it. You've got to pay your debt to society.

Hernando: Yo, the punishment has to fit the crime, honey. I'm as innocent as a tea bag. *(The members of the* Chorus *enter and approach* Hernando. *From behind their backs they produce sabers. They make a sword lock around his neck. They move clockwise around him.* Hernando *pleads with them.)* Give me time to make my peace with this Middle Earth.

Chorus: All right. *(They stop their movements and uncross their sabers.)*

Hernando *kneels over William's body. He takes a piece of paper out of his own shirt pocket, and also a pen. He begins to write his will, using William's body as a desk.*

Hernando: *(Scribbling while speaking.)* If I have done anything wrong, I am sorry. If I must die I leave William my Hispanic heritage. To Trudi I leave my riding skills. To Amanda, who plays the lovely princess, I bequeath my chaste kisses. *(To the* Chorus.) I'm finished, you may take me.

Chorus:
>The man who lies there was to commit suicide   his
>third week inside.
>However, he was injured in a fight.
>This put him out of his misery for a while.
>When he woke he struggled for life anew.

>We thank the man who, in a back-handed way,
>   gave William a second wind.

The members of the Chorus *step away from* Hernando *and leave.*

Hernando: Whew! That was a close call. This mistaken identity thing is getting me into way too much trouble. Makes for a long day. It'll be dark soon.

Amanda *gets up from sitting and comes over to them.*

Hernando: It's the Princess of Lilies. She approacheth. *(He bows.)*

Amanda: *(Regally.)* William's in so much trouble, anguish. You are to conduct a vigil around his sick person. For a whole year and a day if it is required. Do not sleep tonight. Death is too near.

Amanda *exits.* William *starts up with a jolt. He is dazed when he speaks.*

William: She was here. Here!

Trudi: Lie down again.

William: Oh, upon the flinty pavement of New Jerusalem the horse treads, exercising, in what is known as a quadrille.

Hernando: *(Making a comforting gesture to him.)* There, there. The Princess arrived with her Lady-in-Waiting. You're to be healed. And escorted back out to the field. *(To himself.)* And I'll joust you down again.

William: The maidens, beautifully costumed, hold their cup to my lips. I drink. These girls, pure as the wind-fanned snow—I'm surprised at my celibacy. Many would say they are nubile, the few would call them nuns.

Trudi: He's not making any sense.

William: Such wonder cannot be described. Its cool beauty makes me want to weep, to cry. The vestal breeze weaves me an invisible garland. Tea is in the air. It uncondemns me, it softens my rage. Let me roam these precincts till all sad thoughts go away.

Hernando: It's that college degree he got in the pen. I wouldn't trust that Empire State College.

William: My description lacks skill, but it's true. I can't talk like the books that that guy brings in on Wednesdays when he comes. He's supposed to be a poet. Let him be what he says he is. (William *stares hard at* Trudi *and* Hernando.) A gathering should not exceed four hours from start to finish. Exception to this rule is made for speaking of dharma and other undefiled conversation.

Trudi: *(To* Hernando.*)* He'll have a lot of adjusting to do.

William: Oh! *(He faints again.)*

Hernando: If we've got to stick around we'll have to figure out a way to pass the time enjoyably.

Trudi: Remember. I know how to use a sword.

The Chorus *is at a side of the playing area.*

Chorus:
   The fading day slinks and begins to sink away.
   Crickets start their chirping.
   The summer night gives way to a fall chill,
   Light a charcoal fire—

A Chorus Member *strikes a match, bends down and lights an imaginary fire. The* Chorus *points to the imaginary fire and continues.*

   Think upon this fire.
   It heats, it boils water,
   It burnishes clay;
   Flickering vessels of life we are,
   Flesh so briefly upon our bones,
   Fears so fast in our hearts;
   Passions so quick to seize what we desire,
   When we are pushed unprepared, away from the
        flame,
   We are left in shock, cooling.
   But we need warmth.

How do we achieve it honestly?
First we must damper worldly expectation down.
Then we must hold our hands to the heat,
Inhale the perfume of the fiery coals,
Listen to their slow broken crackles
And open our eyes.
Ah, we are so blinded with dark gray impatience
That by daybreak we rarely can see
Our own true colors.

Trudi: This camp fire is nice.

Hernando: Nice is relative. It would be nicer if you could *do* something for me. I'm not going to beg for it, though.

The Professor *enters, with a whip in his/her hand.*

Professor:
Everything's relative, except money.
Money is necessary; but not necessarily evil.
There is no evil, except... overpopulation,
Which is yes, actually quite *bad*, if you look at it
From the standpoint of the working class.
For they are forced to devour their brothers and sisters
In a never-ending competition for goods that ensure
    their survival.

Take this schemata, for instance.

The Professor *starts whipping* William.

William: *(While passed out.)* "The host will emerge to invite the guests in. He is poor; the utensils for tea and rice are irregular; the food is plain. The trees and rocks in the garden are simple, as in nature. Any who find this incomprehensible should leave forthwith."

Professor: I'll teach you for taking "Intro to Japanese Culture."

William: *(Groaning, still passed out.)* I'm not your student anymore.

Professor:
But you're my advisee.
"I can be bent,
But I'll never break."
—That's what you all say,
"I can be bent
Just like old Stagger Lee's neck—
When the trapdoor was flung open
His noosed body went down,
Sure, he was stretched a little,
But he danced up off the ground,
Tore away the rope, cleared his throat
And sang the blues once more!"

William: I've graduated. Behind your back.

Professor: That deserves congratulations. *(He whips him more.)* How are these for hermeneutics? Ha, my, this is heuristic!

William: Doesn't a Bachelor's Degree mean anything anymore? *(Swiftly he passes out again.)*

Hernando: *(To the* Professor.) I can't believe they pay you for what you do.

Professor: You're speaking to a man who's been to Boston and Berkeley. You can't treat me like a turkey.

Hernando *begins to drive the* Professor *out.*

Hernando: You don't know nothing about nothing!

Professor: Your English is terrible.

Hernando: My Spanish is no better. Get out! *(He drives the Professor out.)*

Trudi *gazes at* William. *Pause.*

Trudi: His hair was better when it was long.

Hernando: *(Pause. Through with the* Professor. *Returning to* Trudi.) Let's get down to *life*, huh?

Trudi: It's time to rest. *(She finds a smooth spot of ground and lies down on the grass.)*

Hernando: I've heard you say you hated William. That you despised him.

Trudi: You're nosy. You've been listening to Amanda and me.

Hernando: More than listening. *(He bats his eyes.)* You once loved him. Now you say you don't. Or do you? You had a boyfriend most of the time William's been in Stagger Lee. Now your boyfriend's gone. You're thinking William was better than the other guy? Have I got it right? But Billy loves Amanda, so you hide your true feelings from Amanda. You tell her bad things about what William did to you.

Trudi: You and I just work at the same place. Mind your own business. Good-night. No funny stuff, okay?

Hernando: We're not supposed to go to sleep.

Trudi: Right. We'll watch over the situation *you* caused.

Hernando: Not me, man.

Pause. They rest. Hubbub from a distant crowd is heard—the hubbub is made by the Chorus *murmuring loudly. With a jolt,*

William's head and torso rise from the ground. William looks into the distance.

William: No! No. Who are you taking away? *(The hubbub diminishes. The Chorus enters carrying a dead person on a stretcher.)*

Chorus: *(Chanting quicker than before.)*
> Fruit gone.
> Blood less warm.
> How short time is
> After being born.

The Chorus repeats the chant in hushed tones until they retire to the side of the playing area with the stretcher. William speaks while they finish chanting:

William: *(To the Chorus.)*
> He's dead? What happened?
> Did he snitch on somebody or take something?

To himself.

> Your costumes uniform, dark and gray,
> The corpse is an example you hold up to us,
> To show us how awful you think it is to die,
> We already know what it's like to be dead.

The funeral procession passes by and exits. William faints again. Hernando is asleep; he snores. The sounds of crickets are heard. The background music for Hernando's dream starts. The women of the Chorus come in from the side of the playing area.

Chorus: (Women Only.)
> So close to Lake Ontario,
> He can almost hear the waves.
> He *can* hear the waves,

Swelling in, foaming, falling back,
Mixing then with the liquid-belly of life, the lake.
Waves sweeping in, clear blood washing the sand,
Carrying the food, bringing energy,
Like warm tea.

In and out, up and down,
Waves green-blue, star-lit, moon-lit,
In and out, atop the foaming firmament,
Upon a waterbed, upon
Squishy waves, waves on the pillowly, puffy
    inland sea,
The bed is on a ship,
The cabin has clever posters on the walls,
Shining in the florescent black light,
Mirror overhead, massage oils standing by, some
already applied,
Music softly swirls around,
A woman lolls on the cushioned, fleshy, incensed,
    water bed.
More than one woman.
Liquid waves like the waves on the pillowly, puffy
    ocean,
On a ship to heaven, rising in rhythm
Oh, to be in the quim of a woman
On a waterbed on the inland sea,
Ontario, one moans in pleasure,
Ontario.
Let's enter the pleasure cove.

He starts up from his spot on the ground.

Hernando: *(Loudly, but still in his sleep.)* Ooh, that was exquisite, ladies. I'll be ready for you a second time in no time. The ship is momentarily becalmed. Not a taste of northeaster in the air.

Trudi: *(Not asleep.)* Excuse me?

Hernando: I'll go up to the eagle's nest. 'Just shimmy down this hard, stiff mast. Wow, I'm ready so soon again, ladies! Oh, this pole is sturdy! You can depend on me all over again. *(Seeing something. Another dream fragment:)* My God. They're awful close to each other—just to be looking out at the watery waves. God, she's backed up against the railing. What's Trudi doing? She's kissing those sweet pink silver dollars... Let me at them myself. *(Pause. Hernando twists and turns in his sleep.)* Jesus. Her neck, how it gleams. Kiss that thin, sweet nape. Kiss all that naked flesh. I always knew Amanda had a thing for Trudi. *(Pause.)*

Ahoy there, ladies. Fine day we're having. Clothes only irritate the flesh when it's so hot out like this. But we already know that. Don't worry, I haven't seen a thing while I've been, ah... sleeping. Miss Amanda, I'm here to stroke you now, wouldn't want to break the rhythm you've had going.

Trudi: *(Awake, she humors him.)* Where is my love stag?

Hernando: *(In his sleep.)* You know I'm right here, baby. Attending to important matters.

Trudi: Come over here.

Hernando: I'll be with you shortly.

Trudi: Come over here now.

Hernando: Why don't you come over here. Baby, I've already got two on my hands.

Trudi: I want my love stag now.

Hernando: Yes, baby, yes. Of course you do.

Trudi: Now. Now. *(With a husky voice.)* I'm wearing that Renaissance stuff those two girls wear.

Hernando: Can't you wait a minute?

Trudi: No.

Hernando: Does me with two girls turn you on?

Trudi: What would really turn me on would be for you to come over here, scoop me up and give me your Texas longhorn.

Hernando: Okay, all right. Jeez! Excuse me, girls, for just a minute. I'll make it up to you, I will. *(He jumps up off the ground and strips down to only a large, bejeweled, overstuffed jockstrap.)* These females can never get enough.

Trudi: That's why I want you to service William first.

Hernando: William?

Trudi: He needs love.

Hernando: That's sick. I'm not AC-DC. *(To himself.)* This is the last time I'm sleeping out underneath the stars. Look, I'm hot, you're hot. Let's get down. To sizzling the bacon.

Trudi: I'll feed you, fatten you. You'll make a fine stew.

Hernando: What? What do you want to do? I'm a *man!* My sword. *(He feels around the ground and picks up an imaginary sword and holds it up.)* By the power of this and my right hand, I can slay, if I have to, more than twelve men. *(He awakens out of his dream. Embarrassed, he puts his clothes back on and lies down to rest.)*

Music changes. Long Pause. Though they are not supposed to do so, Hernando and Trudi fall asleep. Hernando snores again. Pause. Amanda *enters, and first appears more like some kind of spirit than a person. Music continues.*

Amanda: We live by the lake, heaven for us is across, not up. You come ashore wanting more. We once had a night together—you know what I mean. But that's past.

I got what I wanted. I had no intention of letting it happen again.

I pity you, being in prison. When I'm lonely, I write you.

The music ends. Apparently William *wakes up. He speaks in his normal voice.*

William: I figured from Trudi's letter that you were working here.

Amanda: Didn't I tell you in my postcard?

William: You weren't that specific.

Amanda: It's been very bad, hasn't it—

William: You like to think you have some free choice in the world. You can't even wear your own underwear here.

Amanda: I don't feel particularly free myself. I guess it's the condition of the human race. It's not such a big deal to be on the outside. Freedom consists in being able to choose which corporations you want to make richer. I envy you that you have time to think, to reflect.

William: *Take* time to reflect.

Amanda: What time?

During the following Hernando *discreetly gets up from sleeping and exits. It begins to be clear that* Amanda *is depressed.*

William: There's so much toil.

Amanda: Yes. *(Pause.)* I'm being down, I know. But I'm just being realistic.

William: Yes, yes.

Amanda: *You* never were.

William: Yeah, sure I sold dope. I sold escape. I helped people to dream.

Amanda: And look where it got you.

William: You're so vulnerable sometimes. It touches me.

Amanda: Is that why you want my body, too? You never crossed the border with me—I mean, you never got to my soul. I got what I wanted.

William: After, you were cold.

Amanda: I suppose so.

William: Well, you showed Trudi who had the power.

Amanda: Yeah. *(Long pause.)* Teach me to create another reality. You're sailing through, somehow.

William: It may look like that to you.

Amanda: But when it turns out to be all make-believe, God, how painful it must be. *(Pause.)* You're not afraid, like I am.

William: Oh, I'm afraid. That's why there's tea.

Amanda: To have the spirit of inner solitude accords with the way of tea. But who says the grass is greener on the non-materialistic side?

William: I may not be greener, but it gets me through.

Amanda: You always liked grass. Too bad you didn't like Trudi as much.

William: I'm a little more considerate now.

Amanda: See, there has been some rehabilitation.

William: Yes, write the governor. Tell him the war on drugs has been a psychological success.

Amanda: Sweetheart, goodnight. (*She lies down and goes to sleep.* William *sleeps, but fitfully. He wipes a few tears from his eyes. Pause. Hubbub. The* Chorus *enters carrying a dead person—a mass of sticks—atop a stretcher.*)

Chorus: (*Chanting.*)
    Bones, bones, dry bones,
    Get upset, now they're wet.
    Tears will only get you so far.
    Quiet my child.
    You're not dead yet.
    Unlike this poor soul,
    You're not a final set.
    Don't bring on the ghost yet.
    Bones. Bones. Bones...

The Chorus *repeats "Bones" in hushed tones.*

William: No! No.

The Chorus's funeral procession passes by and departs. Hernando comes in. He has a metal detector trained to the ground..

Hernando: Well, it's morning. Up and at 'em. Get ready for another day at the Renaissance fair. Two more weeks here. Then we move the whole kit and caboodle to someplace west of Ashtabula, Ohio. Get those city folks out to the country. Put 'em in touch with what they imagine they once were.

Almost time to get the horses from the stable. Us heroes got to ride on something. *(To* William, *asleep.)* Hey, you, William the Conqueror. Rise and shine. You're a hero, man. You've survived the ordeal. I say, rise. The mind follows that which it loves. Go follow her. (Hernando *goes out. The others start to wake up.)*

William: I must be the first one up. Okay, where's the latrine? *(He gets up and heads off in the opposite direction to where* Hernando *exited.* Amanda *and* Trudi *wake up.)*

Amanda: It takes a lot of guts to sleep under the stars when there's a guy like Hernando around.

Trudi: Well, there's two of us. Safety in numbers. We proved to him we're not afraid.

Amanda: Afraid? I didn't sleep that well.

Trudi: Are you worried that you haven't found another job after this?

Amanda: Maybe I missed something. Where's the paper? *(She sees the newspaper.)* There. *(She looks through it.)* I thought I looked at everything.

Trudi: *(To herself.)* Yeah, all twelve horoscopes.

Amanda: Attention: Financial and Accounting Job Seekers. *(She puts down the paper.)* I'm just not interested. I guess I'll go on to Ohio with the fair.

Trudi: You told you would.

Amanda: A woman should always keep open the option to change her mind.

Trudi: I was just thinking. William is going to be getting out in a month.

Amanda: What made you think of that?

Trudi: I don't know. *(Pause.)* How I stay his friend even though he writes you more is beyond me.

Amanda: He's never to know I have a boyfriend.

Trudi: I don't know how he found out I had one for a while there. *(She looks suspiciously at* Amanda.)

William *enters.*

William: Well, good morning ladies. *(Looks up to the sky.)* A fine bright sun.

Trudi: Speak of the devil.

William: I'd like to celebrate my release with a meal at the Anchor Bar. You're both invited. Then I would like to proceed to Canada. For many years I've looked across the lake, thought about getting there.

Amanda: What would you like to do in Toronto, William?

William: Oh, no, not Toronto. We're going east around the lake. To Ottawa.

Trudi: Can't we just do something in Rochester?

William: No, no. It's time to cross the border. I've read about an exhibition that's visiting the National Gallery—in Ottawa. It's a special treat—all the way from Japan.

Amanda: I have things to do on this side of the border.

William: Don't tell me you have a boyfriend. Someone as good looking as you is bound to. But come on. Come with me. We'll have breakfast on the way.

The women get up and exit with William. *The* Chorus *enters.*

Chorus:
 When man is contrite and has paid his price,
 Grief still resonates throughout his body,
 Turn from the gloom to feel the brightness of this
  moment:

The Chorus *recites the following Japanese verse. An English translation is provided, but it is not to be spoken.*

O-cha, o-cha.	*Honorable tea, honorable tea.*
Kumo mo mayowanu	*On the waves*
Nami no ue ni.	*Where no clouds wander.*
O-cha, o-cha.	*Honorable tea, honorable tea.*

Wounds of bondage are real,
But there are other ways to feel.

O-cha, o-cha.
Kumo mo mayowanu
Nami no ue ni.
O-cha, o-cha.

Peace can be found.

We walk, we arrive, we see.

Bells are heard. Pause. William *and* Trudi *enter.*

Trudi: Wow! We're in Ottawa.

Chorus:
>It's kind of a funny place, this Ottawa.
>Lots of bricks.
>Kind of low-slung.
>Not so bluesy.
>Kind of super clean.
>What a perfect place
>For a visitor,
>An accommodating place
>For the Japanese Tea ritual.

Briefly, the sound of a shakuhachi—a Japanese "flute"— is heard.

William: *(Whispering slightly to* Trudi.*)* It's impossible to estimate what an important role the tea ritual has played on shaping Japanese culture.

Trudi: *(Also trying to be quiet.)* It looks like the demonstration is about to start up again.

William: *(Quietly.)* People dedicate their whole lives to the Way of Tea. It's a world transformed.

Trudi: Amanda should have come along. She doesn't know what she's missing.

William: Ah, yes, well, Amanda...

The Tea Master *enters dressed in a simple Japanese costume. She is carrying two straw mats. She spreads the mats out on the ground.* William *and* Trudi *stand off to the side looking. After the* Tea Master *has smoothed out the mats, her female*

Tea Assistant, *played by* Hernando, *walks in with minced steps. He is wearing feminine make up and wears a florid kimono. He carries a portable brazier* (furo), *a tea kettle* (kama), *a lacquered board, and a small container containing tea leaves. Underneath his costume he is still Hernando; he always uses his "own" voice.*

Hernando: Oh, man, I've never been so restricted in movement in my entire life. Whoever thought up this kind of thing was out of his gourd.

Trudi: *(Softly, laughing, to* William.) I think it was a man, Hernando.

Hernando: *(To* Trudi *and* William.) Why are you talking like you're T.V. announcers at a golf match? *(To the* Tea Master.) Here's your bloody accouterments, most honorable lady tea master.

Tea Master: *Arigato go-zaimasu. (To All.)* You may speak with a normal voice but not of normal things. Our setting generates a charged field of emptiness divested of worldly appetites.

Hernando: Christ. I'll have to get the tea-bowls. Why don't they just slam me in the family jewels, instead of making me wear this. *(He exits to get the bowls.)*

Tea Master: One seeks to create in tea the affirmative core of the life of the hermit in his unpretentious thatched hut.

William: The spirit of the tea ceremony is exemplified by the expression "harmony, reverence, purity and tranquillity."

Tea Master: When we make tea we are struck by the wonder of our own existence.

Trudi: This is Zen, isn't it?

LANCE TAIT

William: Yes.

Trudi: Intro to Japanese Culture. I would've thought you'd study this in it.

Tea Master: We break down the perception that things stand as materials apart from the self. In tea, things cease to appear as discrete, enduring objects of desire—or aversion. We are not separate souls, nor individuals. We are one. We seek to attain the Tendai concept of "One Mind", a single instant of thought that is not divided from all things and in which things are perceived nonhierarchically. *(Pause.)*

Before you have come here you have contemplated the landscape gardens, the painted scrolls on the walls. Also the flower arrangement, and the willow branches beside— everything that coexists in a harmonious relationship with the entire ceremony.

While the Chorus *intones the following, the* Tea Master *sets the brazier in place on the lacquered board. She carefully places the tea kettle on the board. Note: the English translation is not to be recited by the* Chorus.

Chorus:

O-cha, o-cha.	*Honorable tea, honorable tea.*
Omou mi-nori no	*The dharma I seek*
Tomosureba	*Not to defile*
Yo wataru hashi to	*Becomes a bridge*
Nami no ue ni.	*For making my way in the world.*
O-cha, o-cha.	*Honorable tea, honorable tea.*

Tea Master:
Honorable Tea,
The dharma I seek

284 •

Not to defile
Becomes a bridge
For making my way in the world.
Honorable Tea.

In tea, we fuse the mundane and the transcendent. Common objects and elemental acts of everyday life acquire a wholeness and transparency. Sincerity is necessary; freedom from intent to impress is also. Spontaneity surprises us gladly, even though the objects are arranged "just so". *(Pause.)* Ah, our intellect does not grasp what we do.

I have arranged the ashes thusly: at the front and back of the ash I have make two parallel mountain ridges. Some white ash has been sprinkled on the "mountains" to suggest coolness.

Let me tell you about coolness: first, do not take for granted that you will be alive in the morning. Remember that all problems arise from our anxious clinging to life. Coolness stands in contrast to youthful exuberance and vitality. We appreciate the cold of the hermit's hut in autumn, the ice outside in winter; and especially the chill of the water in the water-jar before it is boiled for tea.

Even though it is summer we still think of coolness: for it resides at the roots of the spruce, where the crystalline stream wells up. Ah, how the mention of autumnal waters brings a brisk clarity to the mind. The world with its clamorous surface loses our attentions. What holds us is the muted and the unadorned. Our desires no longer burn. We seem to die while we are alive. Feeling for all things is awakened in us. We attain the One Mind. The world is perceived in its profundity and mystery. Tea helps us to this.

Chorus:
> O-cha, o-cha.
> Omou mi-nori no
> Tomosureba
> Yo wataru hashi to
> Nami no ue ni.
> O-cha, o-cha.

Tea Master: You may cross the tearoom diagonally to inspect. Please. *(She gestures to* William *and* Trudi. *They cross diagonally.)* Examine the brazier, the kettle, and the ash. Under the three pieces of burning charcoal initially placed in the brazier, the trigram for water from the *Yi Jing* has been written in the ash. Thus metal, wood, earth, fire and water—the five elements—are all present.

Now you make a slight genuflection. You do not fully bow. Never let formal etiquette replace spiritual feeling. (William *and* Trudi *half-bow.)*

The guests go to the utensil area now. The more experienced are allowed to touch them. They touch them with their hearts, not just their hands. After admiring the utensils, we close the door loudly to signal that all are present. After the tea-bowls arrive, arrangement will be completed.

The air of tranquillity is broken by a short scream that comes from "off stage."

Tea Master: *(Continuing as if she had heard nothing.)* The tea will be prepared in absolute silence. However, you shall expect the Three Sounds of Tea: first, the clink of the lid on the kettle; second, the tap of the tea-bowl on the mat; third, the clink of the teaspoon on the tea-bowl. Your feelings, of grace perhaps, may be shared by all, who are now one.

There is a scream again. It is Hernando *who is screaming. He comes out with a bed sheet wrapped around himself—he has bled all over it. His lips have been bloodied, smeared with blood to make him look like he is wearing lots of lipstick. He screams in anguish,. The* Flags Man *comes in. Pause. The* Flags Man *reads from script pages on a clipboard.*

Flags Man: Confusions previous to Stagger Lee Prison not allowed to stand. The facts beforehand—county client Subject Number 1: Hispanic. By the name of Hernando Sanpaio-Cortez. A strutter. Report: While the guards were occupied with the flooding in the lockup after a big storm, jail inmates dressed him up in long dress made from bed sheets. They knocked him around.

William: *(Pleading, in the manner of a peace-maker.)* It's his culture, man. Don't blame him, I don't blame him. It's in his culture. No one's sane when they're behind bars.

Flags Man: *(Reading.)* They bloodied his lips for lipstick. Made him walk and talk like a girl. Subject Number 2: A white man named Joseph Benner. Subject Number 3: A black man named Charles Sontag. Clarification: these last two men, who like to be called Scarecrow Joe and Plantation Charles, respectively, forced their way upon Subject Number 1. They enjoyed their butt sports and said that would learn him for being such a peacock.

Hernando, *wounded, cries out in anguish.*

Trudi: Oh, God.

Hernando: I'm innocent. I've always been innocent.

The Flags Man *supports* Hernando. Hernando *limps out, and the* Flags Man *exits with him.*

Tea Master: *(Continuing as if nothing happened.)* We know that the cleaning of all the dishes and utensils that meet the tea symbolize a cleansing and purification of the mind.

William: *(Upset.)* The stillness, the emptiness. Don't you know I'm jumping out of my skin? I want wind. Rain. There's a storm inside. I want one outside too. Blow winds! Rage, damn it. Rage! Blow—*(Quickly, thunder sounds. We hear sounds of a raging storm. William breaks down and cries.)* I can't take it anymore!

The Chorus *marches in with the "dead man" sticks on a stretcher as before.*

Chorus Member: *(Spoken by the actor who plays the Herald.)* You've said that before.

Chorus: *(Chanting.)*
Bones, bones, dry bones,
Get upset, they'll be wet.
Tears will only get you so far.
Quiet my child.
You're not dead yet.
Unlike this poor soul,
You're not a final set.
Don't bring on the ghost yet.
Bones. Bones. Bones...

The din of the storm subsides.

Whatever the situation
Remember at least you got an education.

Softer chanting, the same rhythm:

Bones. Bones. Bones. Bones... *(Etc.)*

The storm ends. The Chorus *almost marches off. He stops them.*

William: No, wait. I'm not going to cry. *(He looks simply at the actors with deep appreciation. He embraces each of the actors.)* Thank you for being my thoughts. *(He goes to a* Chorus Member *and embraces him or her.)* It's the arrangement of things that will help me through.

Chorus: *(Marching in place.)* Bones, bones, bones, bones.

William: Don't go. It's very kind of you. Please, don't move. The positions you're standing in are just right. They make me feel... at one with you, with the world... I don't know how else to put it. Thank you for being the entire diplomatic corps from the land of dreams. I'm deeply indebted to you.

The women of the Chorus *stop marching in place.*

Chorus: (Women Only.)
Tra-la-la-la-la, la-la,
Renaissance Fair.

Chorus: *(All members, marching in place, chanting.)*
Bones, bones, bones, bones.
Rain gone. Fruit gone.
How short the time of bloom,
How long
The time for things to go wrong.

William: Don't leave just yet. I told you I'm completely in your debt. I don't mean to cling... but you're of the universe ...and the rest is... well it's just a very sick state of affairs for some people that feel so apart.

Trudi: *(Reassuring him.)* You really will get out of prison someday soon.

Chorus: *(Marching in place.)* Bones, bones, bones, bones... *(With stretcher in hand, they march out, chanting:)*

Bones, bones, bones, bones... *(Etc.)*

Tea Master: I'm sorry, but I must go, too.

The Tea Master *exits. The* Actress *and the* Flags Man *come in. The* Flags Man *has his cart with him.*

Actress: It went pretty well, I think. Have you met our man with the flags?

William: No. How... how are you?

Flags Man: Hello.

They shake hands.

William: Oh, and thank *you.*

Actress: It was our pleasure to do this play.

William: If I hadn't read so much I wouldn't think that such a thing like this could be possible. *(He notices an* actor *in the "just off stage"* Chorus. *He brings him out.)* You did a fine job playing the Professor. Thank you. You were wonderful. *(He looks over at the* Chorus, *then:)* So were all of you. *(To the* Chorus member *that plays the* Professor.) Please let me shake your hand. *(He looks over at the* Chorus, *then:)* All of your hands. Please, don't move. The way you're standing now—relaxed as a branch of leaves—boy, it calms my soul. I tell you, I'm deeply honored. *(He looks over at the* Chorus *with admiration.)*

Flags Man: Weird.

William: Thank you, Trudi. You've been a good friend to me. I don't deserve it.

William *goes over to some of the* Chorus *members and shakes their hands.* Trudi *goes over and greets them as well. Long pause.*

Flags Man: Very weird. *(To the* Actress.) Is he in prison? Or what?

Actress: Ask him.

Flags Man: It's obvious he doesn't know. Hmm. What's the point here? The whole thing kind of moved funny.

Actress: The point's to get through the story—quickly, with great style. And it worked. I don't think we lost the audience.

Flags Man: But something's wrong. It's all odd. It's kind of... free.

Actress: Makes you wonder, doesn't it?

Flags Man: I'm glad I'm not in prison. Most people aren't—you said this was supposed to be a universal story.

Trudi: *(From over by the* Chorus.) Well, it covers a few corners in the world, isn't that enough?

Flags Man: Well, it did get around a little. Why did it have to be the way it was?

Actress: *(Protesting.)* It was lively, wasn't it?

Flags Man: Yeah, sure. *(Pause.)* Hey, how'd I do?

William *and* Trudi *are by now finished with their "visiting with" the* Chorus. *The* Chorus *moves towards the stretcher of sticks.*

Actress: Oh. Your acting was superb.

LANCE TAIT

Flags Man: I bet you say that to everybody.

Actress: *(Aside.)* Actually, I do.

The Chorus *starts chanting; they hoist up the stretcher with sticks arranged on it as before.* William and Trudi *both stand aside as the* Chorus *moves into the playing area with the stretcher.*

Chorus: *(Chanting.)*
Bones, bones, bones,
Don't get upset,
You're not dead yet.
Unlike this poor soul,
You're not a final set.
Don't bring on the ghost yet.
Bones. Bones. Bones...

The Chorus *marches in place. While the* Chorus *repeats the words "Bones" chanting on the downbeat of a 2-beat measure—and often resting their voices on various measures, the dialogue continues:*

Actress: Well, I'm gonna have to be going.

Flags Man: So am I.

Actress: Thanks for your help. *(They shake hands.)*

Flags Man: 'Be seeing you.

Actress: Bye.

Each go off in their separate directions. With William *and* Trudi *looking on, the* Chorus *marches in place, chanting "Bones" occasionally, and always on top of the beat. Their chanting and marching dies down; the play comes to an end.*

Acknowledgments

In addition to Yvonne Shafer, Frank Hoff and those already mentioned in the previous pages, I would like to thank the many actors that acted in these plays. I would also like to thank Bruce Boswell for assistance with book design and word-processing; Linda Jones at Enfield Publishing; among those at Bard College: Robert Rockman, Elie Yarden, Ben Boretz, Justus Rosenberg; the Taits and John Murphy; Gordon Rogoff; Derek Walcott and Boston University; Domenico Pietropaolo, Colin Visser and the University of Toronto; Robert Orchard, Arthur Holmberg and the American Repertory Theatre; Marc Kozak for book design; Joseph Meeker, John Tallmadge and the Union Institute, Cincinnati; Martin Lockley, Bill Troop, Gail Elwell, Wanda Ivey, Linda Tyrol; Yves and Sophie Gaudin; Lucy and Julian Cook, John and Chris Thomas; Brad Bowles and the University of Colorado at Denver; Patrick Barrows, the Segarnicks, Jean Hoff, the Motsingers, Chris and Laurie Brown.